SPIRITUAL SLUMBER

Awaken Your Spiritual Sensitivity to Overcome Destiny Swappers and Evil Exchangers

DR. ANTHONIA ADEYEYE

Spiritual Slumber

Copyright © 2025 Dr. Anthonia Adeyeye
Paperback ISBN: 978-1-965593-66-0

No part of this publication may be reproduced, distributed, or transmitted in any form or by any means, including photocopying, recording, or other electronic or mechanical methods, without the prior written permission of the publisher, except in the case of brief quotations embodied in critical reviews and specific non-commercial uses permitted by copyright law.

Scripture quotations are taken from the Holy Bible (AMP, NIV, ESV, NKJV, and MSG). Any references to specific Scriptures are for educational or illustrative purposes only.

Published by Cornerstone Publishing

A Division of Cornerstone Creativity Group LLC
Info@thecornerstonepublishers.com
www.thecornerstonepublishers.com

Author's Contact

To order bulk copies of this book, please write to:
Dr. Anthonia Adeyeye
Adeyeye Evangelistic Ministries (AEM)
P.O. Box 810, West Hempstead, NY 11552
drfestus@alcministries.com

Printed in the United States of America.

DEDICATION

To the children of Mr. and Mrs. Sloppy and all the victims of spiritual slumber. May God give light to your eyes.

CONTENTS

DEDICATION iii
ACKNOWLEDGMENTS vii
INTRODUCTION ix

1. The Sleep of Death 1
2. Awaken from Your Slumber 9
3. While Men Slept! 17
4. The Prostitute and Her Sleep of Death 33
5. Deliverer Demoted to a Grinder of Grains 47
6. David Versus the Killer in King's Clothing 53
7. Parents, Reject the Sleep of Death! 61
8. Take Action 75
9. Examples of Some Spiritually Alert Women 81

10. Examples of People Who Slept the Sleep of Death....95

11. Practical Ways to Prevent the Sleep of Death....107

12. Special Prayers Against the Sleep of Death 135

CONCLUSION 166

ACKNOWLEDGMENTS

Firstly, my gratitude goes to the Lord, who inspired me to write this book. God stirred me and helped to unstuck me when I hit the wall. Thank you, my father, for giving light to my eyes when it seemed like I had fallen into spiritual slumber.

My forever appreciation goes to my pastor, Dr. Festus Adeyeye, the G.O. of the end-time harvests. Thank you for being my pastor, father, teacher, and mentor. I am pleased to ignite my light from your light. Your light will never be dim but shine to light the world for Christ.

I am eternally grateful to all my children, especially the girls. Thank you for always encouraging me with your nice words, beautiful smiles, challenging queries, and questions. Of course, I love my guys dearly! Sometimes, I wonder how you all grew up so fast! I love you all one by one, and I will never trade you for all the riches in the world. Also, a big thank you goes to our five and growing-in-number grandchildren. Thank you for being in my world. You bring smiles to my face all the time.

Furthermore, I appreciate my siblings (Niyi, Femmy, and Jay). We have been through the ups and downs of life together. We have weathered thick and thin; thank you for always coming together to pray. God bless you and your amazing families. Also, special hugs to my triplets; Pum, Pressy, and Bimbola. Thank you for always being there!

Lastly, my sincere appreciation goes to my ALCC family. You mean what the Word of God says in the Message Bible version of Proverbs 18:24 (MSG): *"Friends come and friends go, but a true friend sticks by you like family."* Thank you, ALCC, for being my family! To all my families and friends all over the world - thank you for being there for me. Blessings upon blessings to you all.

To Tolulope (my editor), my proofreader, and all those who made it possible for this book to hit the print, you will forever enjoy God's favor.

Thank you, everyone!

INTRODUCTION

For everyone, sleeping time is a time of refreshing, off from the day's activities. It should be an enjoyable time to rejuvenate for the next day. However, our adversary, the devil, uses this period to operate and destroy the lives of people.

Spiritual slumber, in this context, is referred to in the Bible as the *"sleep of death."* Although the overarching theme of this book is spiritual slumber; that subtle drift into complacency, drowsiness, and dullness of spirit that makes us easy prey for destiny swappers and evil exchangers - you will see me adopt the term *"sleep of death"* in subsequent chapters to align more precisely with Scripture's language and urgency.

When the Holy Spirit quickened my spirit to write this book, it became more apparent that the more I understood the subject matter, the more I realized that I have been a victim of the sleep of death many times. I was not just a victim some years back; I have experienced the sleep of death as recently as the time of writing this book. I believe that as you read this book, you will have a clearer understanding of this dangerous condition, its signs, and its consequences.

Many years ago, while pregnant with one of our children, I had a terrible dream. I was lying down on a hospital bed and saw an older woman whom I recognized very well. The woman tied my legs to the rails of the bed, and my legs were widely opened as if I was going to deliver the baby. Then, this woman took a loaded syringe and emptied it inside of me. Unfortunately, I watched her do this evil act, and I did not fight to resist her at all! This was very unlike me, as I have always prayed to God to give me a fighting, aggressive, and destructive spirit against the kingdom of darkness.

In a normal circumstance, I would have fought her and prevented her from releasing the liquids into me. Unfortunately, she did, and I woke up immediately, with excruciating abnormal pain, as I was approaching delivery of the baby! I woke my husband and narrated my experience, and this led to an intense session of prayer. While we were still praying, I suddenly had the urge to vomit. I rushed to the toilet and vomited out darkish substances, and the stomachache stopped immediately!

This was, indeed, a great deliverance! Supposing God was not gracious to me by giving me the grace to be alert to remember the dream and the wisdom to quickly address the dream spiritually, the outcome would have been different.

When you understand the subject matter of this book, you will agree that anyone, no matter the spiritual maturity and intimacy with God, can become a victim. The main issue is not only being a victim but also knowing the antidotes and preventive measures.

It is my sincere prayer that as you read this book, you will have a better understanding of spiritual slumber, and how it is revealed in Scripture as the sleep of death - including how to prevent it, and how to conquer it when it occurs. May the Holy Spirit, the Teacher Himself, give us all continuous insights into the things of the Spirit. Through this book, you will be delivered and learn how to be fortified to prevent Satan from infiltrating your sleep time for his evil agendas.

Come with me as we unravel this dangerous, often underestimated condition and learn how to awaken fully in the spirit.

CHAPTER ONE

The Sleep of Death

It's already well-known that Satan is the arch-enemy of mankind, and he carries out his three-fold ministry of stealing, killing, and destroying at all times. Truthfully, he carries out his evil acts when men are asleep, and this, of course, will lead us to a clear definition of what the sleep of death is.

> "*24 Jesus gave them another parable [to consider], saying, "The kingdom of heaven is like a man who sowed good seed in his field. 25 But while his men were sleeping, his enemy came and sowed [c]weeds [resembling wheat] among the wheat, and went away. 26 So when the plants sprouted and formed grain, the weeds appeared also. 27 The servants of*

> *the owner came to him and said, 'Sir, did you not sow good seed in your field? Then how does it have weeds in it?'* [28] *He replied to them, An enemy has done this."* (Matthew 13:24-28, AMP)

Sleeping the sleep of death can be defined as when a person is physically sleeping, probably in a semi-conscious state, and outrageous things are done to the person or their loved ones, and the person is incapacitated or helpless to stop the evil act.

Sleeping the sleep of death can also be a state of lukewarmness or coldness in the Spirit. This occurs when a person is not spiritually alert, and Satan takes advantage to carry out his three-fold evil ministry. This situation implies that an individual could be tired and resting, and evil acts are performed against such a person while physically asleep.

The sleep of death could also refer to a state where a person is awake but is oblivious or helpless to the dangerous things influencing their life.

Another definition of the sleep of death can be found in Psalm 90:5-6 (NIV): *"*[5] *Yet you sweep people away in the sleep of death—they are like the new grass of the morning:* [6] *In the morning it springs up new, but by evening it is dry and withered."*

The sleep of death can also be referred to as the condition of sweeping away mentally, spiritually, or even physically. It involves being insensitive towards the events and situations around them.

Additionally, the sleep of death is also when people, Christians, intellectualize spiritual matters. This happens when Christians incorrectly and or even ignorantly analyze or provide scientific answers or personal opinions to the things of the Spirit. For example, the dream I shared earlier in the introductory part of this book would be incorrectly intellectualized and interpreted as either a bad dream or stomach upset, and the vomitus could have been a result of a bad dinner.

The Bible made it clear in 1 Corinthians 2:14 (ESV): *"The natural person does not accept the things of the Spirit of God, for they are folly to him, and he is not able to understand them because they are spiritually discerned."*

It is clear from the Scripture that if you are not sensitive to the Holy Spirit and live naturally, you won't understand the things of the Spirit and will therefore analyze the situation rather than reflect to know the next action to take.

According to the parable of the sower in Matthew 13:24-28, God was the owner of the field, and He sowed good seeds and put His men in charge. But something happened thereafter. Verse 25 says, *"But while **his men were sleeping**, his enemy came and sowed [c] weeds [resembling wheat] among the wheat, and went away."* This implies that His men were not alert; they were sleeping the sleep of death. This kind of sleep is what people engage in, and terrible things are done to them or the things/people belonging to them. In this situation, they are passive or inactive until the enemy successfully carries out his evil works.

The question you should be asking now is, "So, who is this enemy?"

The Bible says, in the same verse 25 that the man's enemy came and sowed tares resembling wheat. The enemy of the man is Satan. Satan hates God, and from the beginning of time, Satan has constantly thwarted the plans of God. In the illustrated Scripture, it was not the man who was asleep but his men. Our God can never sleep, and He does not grow weary.

God has already given the dominion of the world to humanity. Your responsibility is to guard whatever God has given to you, because Satan, the adversary, goes around the whole world, always looking for someone he can devour (1 Peter 5:8). You should know by now that God is good because He created man in His image and likeness and has great plans for His creatures. So, if someone is killing, destroying, and stealing around you, such a person is the devilish one - Satan.

Satan is the one who corrupts and defiles God's plans in the lives of people. He has varied ways of performing his evil havoc. One major way he sows evil seeds in peoples' destinies is when people are physically sleeping, spiritually sluggish, or spiritually ignorant. When they are tired and asleep, Satan comes through dreams to steal, kill, and destroy the destinies of men and thwart God's plans for their lives. In this parable, the people were deep in slumber, and the man's enemy sowed weeds to thwart the bountiful harvests of the seed sown.

The weeds that Satan sows into the lives of people are premature death, sicknesses, afflictions, stagnation, dryness, hatred, family confusion and divisions, divorce, depression, discouragement, lies against God and other people, and fear; the list of Satan's havoc is inexhaustible.

ENJOYING THE ABUNDANT LIFE THAT GOD GIVES

Jesus said in John 10:10 (NKJV), *"The thief does not come except to steal, and to kill, and to destroy. I have come that they may have life, and that they may have it more abundantly."* This sentence is loaded with many facts, and I will explain the deduction in this verse.

1. The Thief Comes

No matter your personality, astuteness, or economic buoyancy, the thief (Satan) has no respect for such. He will come in different ways, through different means, and one of the means is the subject being discussed in this book. Satan comes to attack people through dreams when they are asleep and spiritually vulnerable. By the grace of God, you will be empowered to fortify the spirit, soul, and body against the wiles of Satan. Even if the devil still comes, a mature Christian will know that nothing will come out of the attacks, because the Christian is spiritually combative and will stand strong until victory is achieved.

2. Jesus Came to Give People Life

Jesus said, *"I have come that they may have life."* Naturally, one may think everyone alive has life. However, from this sentence, a person may be alive and is just existing but not experiencing the real life of God - ZOE, which is the fullness of living and enjoying life instead of being alive and enduring life. Some people are alive, but a good picture of their existence can be likened to when Joseph was alive, but in prison (Genesis 40), living below the standard of life God intended for him to live.

Enduring life can also be likened to when Lazarus came out of the grave, but his eyes, hands, and feet were still bound! Jesus restored Lazarus to the fullness of life.

The eyes must see, feet must move, and hands must be productive. I pray that you will experience the yoke-destroying and bondages-removing power of God in Jesus' name. As Jesus freed the eyes of Lazarus to see, his feet to walk, and his hands to be productive, you are restored and made whole in Jesus' name. May you walk in the light of God and enjoy the fullness of living and the freeness of life. The power of God removes your name from the list of life "endurers."

If you are not already enjoying the fullness of life Jesus came to give us, the way God intends it, you will begin to do so by the power in the name of Jesus. If you are already enjoying the Zoe—the life of God, you will even enjoy such life to the overflow, much more abundantly.

One of the ways Satan steals the abundant living from people is to cause them to slumber, to sleep deep sleep, and all kinds of the sleep of death, when they are supposed to be awake and alert. I pray that as you read this masterpiece, you will be delivered from the various schemes that Satan devises during people's slumber. I pray grace be released upon your spirit to be aggressive, dangerous, destructive, and combative when you are asleep or awake. There is the power of God in all Christians to make us spiritually combative and not sluggish — the power of God that makes a destiny to be delivered, no matter how badly they have been wounded, the power that sets the captives free and turns captivity around. The power that solves long problems and destroys family foundational strongholds of darkness is the power of God.

Brethren, it is time to start enjoying the good sleep that God ordained for you. Your period of sleep is supposed to be a time of refreshing and healing, not a time of affliction and destruction of destinies. I pray that anyone whose destiny has been injured, wounded, or afflicted, including those who have fallen flat along the rails of life due to the sleep of death, will arise and utter the prayers in this book continuously to experience total deliverance in Jesus' name.

Psalm 127:2 (AMP) says, *"It is vain for you to rise early, To retire late, To eat the bread of anxious labors—For He gives [blessings] to His beloved even in his sleep."*

This particular verse, in many Bible versions, concludes the last few words as "God gives His beloved sleep." This is very true, and we all know that God does not give anything evil. He gives every good and perfect gift (James 1:17). In addition to giving His beloved good sleep, He adds His sweetness and blessings to the sleep. Therefore, I affirm God's promise of sweet sleep upon you; you will not sleep the sleep of death.

CHAPTER TWO

Awaken from Your Slumber

By the power of the Holy Spirit, I have come to understand that there are three types of the sleep of death, though there may still be more types. So, let's explore the three types:

1. The first type occurs when a person is physically sleeping and having nightmares of good things being successfully taken from their body, life, or family. The person may be passive or inactive while the havoc of stealing, killing, or destroying is being done in such dreams.

2. The second type of sleep of death is when a person sleeps and dies in the sleep or shortly after having bad dreams of death.

The Bible says in Psalm 90:5 (NIV), *"Yet you sweep people away in the sleep of death."* In this case, victims are swept away prematurely from the land of the living. Some may die even while sleeping. I am not insinuating that all who died while sleeping died only through the sleep of death, as it is being discussed in this book. However, many have died not through natural causes or medical challenges, but through the evil atrocities of men and the devil. Many people have died untimely after having bad dreams of being shot or killed. Some were attacked while asleep and probably did not take it up spiritually as they should have taken it, and this resulted in their untimely deaths.

3. The third kind of sleep of death that the Lord opened my eyes to see is the one that a victim does not need to be physically sleeping. This is the sleep of death when people are swept away mentally or spiritually. People lose their minds and are not sensitive to paying attention to the happenings in their lives or around them. I coined this type of sleep of death — mental slumber, spiritual slumber, or the sleep of death. The devil comes in to cause damage in their lives due to their insensitivities to the things of the Spirit.

The sleep of death is also the spirit of slumber, in which the Christian is spiritually careless and too lazy to observe the happenings around them and the gifts of God in their lives until bad things start to happen. In this situation, the enemy takes advantage to cause problems, mysteries, and difficulties in their lives.

GENERALLY, THE SLEEP OF DEATH IS CHARACTERIZED BY:

1. Victims who are passive or inactive and do not fight back while they are being attacked, manipulated, or oppressed in their dreams. The victim may dream of good destinies being vandalized, manipulated, and changed to substandard destinies. Still, the victim will observe these atrocities and will not do anything to fight back in the dream.

2. The dreamer who sees figures or people that I call satanic operators. They come into the person's dream and introduce a sickness, affliction, or negativity into the dreamer's life. The dreamer sees everything but does little or nothing to confront the attacker.

3. Dreams that reveal an evil agenda that Satan wants to carry out in the person's life in the future. Sometimes, victims will take revelations or negative information as final, both in the dream and after they awake from sleep. They do not rise to cancel or neutralize the evil

experience, or if they take any step to counteract the dream, their actions could be done through fear and not in faith.

4. Victims who sleep and encounter evil people or figures stealing things from them, feeding them food to eat, or having sex with them, and once they wake up, bad things will start happening in their lives.

5. A dreamer of the sleep of death who may fight an attacker or an evil person in the dream, but if the dream does not end victoriously, it will lead to the dreamer experiencing difficulty in life or the dreamer living a life filled with challenges.

6. Sometimes, people have bad dreams, but it is their loved ones or people they know who were attacked, oppressed, or afflicted, but they were not able to help in the dream. In reality, their loved ones or relatives (seen in the dream) may start experiencing hardship and afflictions. Such people are sleeping the sleep of death because they could have attacked the attackers in their dreams, but they never did. Although they are not the direct victims of the wickedness of men, they do not stand in the gap to cover their loved ones, relatives, and the people seen in their dreams.

7. Periods when Satan and evil people will manipulate people into the sleep of death by "appearing as

friends or loved ones of their victims." These satanic people will come to you in dreams as the faces of the people you love and trust.

I had a dream of such a thing, in which one of my biological sisters offered me my favorite food. This person who "posed" or masqueraded as my biological sister even called me by my pet name. To God be the glory, the Holy Spirit did not permit me to accept the food offered to me. He showed me that the food was poisoned and that the person I saw was not my sister! Of course, it was not my real sister that appeared to me in this sleep. It was Satan, using people and things familiar to me, such as my favorite food and a wonderful sister whom Satan knew I would not refuse any offer from.

Wicked people masquerade in this fashion to confuse you about the people in your life. When wicked men appear using familiar spirits or people, they know that you will not fight these people both in real life and in your dreams because you trust them. So, they will successfully implement their evil agendas unhindered because victims have been deceived. Additionally, Satan uses this method to confuse the relationships of people you trust, so the victim is blinded, fighting the wrong people and battles. The person will be fighting friends and loved ones as enemies while the wicked people get away and will continue to cause damage. However, it takes the Holy Spirit and being sensitive to not take friends as enemies and enemies as friends. Your spiritual eyes must not be blinded; they must be opened. You must not sleep the sleep of death in this manner.

There are many examples of people in the Bible who slept the sleep of death, and some struggled through life, while some even died. As it was in the old times, so it is today. Some individuals are sleeping the sleep of death; although they are alive, they are living a life filled with mysteries, difficulties, frustrations, and hardships.

There was the case of a lady who always saw a woman in her dreams every time she was pregnant. This woman would not come to appear to her in the dream until this dear lady became pregnant. Once this older lady appeared to this lady, she would feed the younger lady with some kind of food, and the pregnancies would come down immediately in torrential flows of blood! This is an example of what the sleep of death is — when people are asleep and good things are stolen from them countless times.

As I have mentioned earlier in the introduction part, I have also experienced this phenomenon of the sleep of death, even as a Christian. Although I was a tongue-speaking, Bible-reading, and praying Christian, the devil almost destroyed the blessing of God in my life through spiritual insensitivity. It was a sleep of death on my part — the kind of sleep whereby a valuable thing is stolen or something bad takes place, and the victim cooperates or makes things easy for the perpetrators.

It is my sincere prayer that the Holy Spirit will give you more understanding and awaken you from your slumber as you proceed further in the book.

CHAPTER THREE

While Men Slept!

Jesus gave a parable in the book of Matthew 13:24-30. However, I will emphasize verses 24-25 for this chapter and this book.

> "*24 Jesus gave them another parable [to consider], saying, "The kingdom of heaven is like a man who sowed good seed in his field. 25 But while his men were sleeping, his enemy came and sowed [c]weeds [resembling wheat] among the wheat, and went away."* (Matthew 13:24-25, AMP)

You will notice that the men in this parable were supposed to be watching the field in which the good seeds were sown. Instead of watching, they fell asleep, and the man's enemy came into the field and sowed tares. As discussed in chapter one, victims of the sleep of death may sleep physically, like the men in this parable, or be spiritually sluggish or ignorant. One common thing is that while victims sleep the sleep of death, the enemy takes advantage during the period to sow tares by hurting them or their loved ones. So, let's discuss what the enemy does during this period.

THE ATTACK OF THE ENEMY DURING THE SLEEP OF DEATH

During the sleep of death, the enemy can do the following:

1. The enemy can sow bad seeds, similar to the parable above. In this case, bad things are planted into the victim's body or destiny.

2. The enemy can remove and replace the good things in the life of the victim in exchange for bad things.

3. The enemy can completely remove good things and not replace them with anything.

4. The enemy can distract and dislodge people from their God-ordained destinies.

5. Christians can be spiritually insensitive to the happenings in their lives or the lives of their loved ones. Such insensitivities will lead to the Christians not rising to do the needful to stop the enemy's attack.

6. Satan's evil has no limit, and his evil ministry is to steal, kill, and destroy, as stated in John 10:10a. Satan can carry out any evil within and beyond the expectations of men. The devil can kill, as stated in John 10:10. However, as children of God, with the help of the Holy Spirit, we will not sleep the sleep of death. The devil will not be able to take advantage of anything in us in Jesus' name.

EFFECTS OF THE SLEEP OF DEATH

Consequences of the sleep of death include, but are not limited to the following:

1. Delays in realizing the promises and plans of God.
2. Hardship of life.
3. Sudden turning of a good life or situation to bad after a dream or an occurrence of the sleep of death.
4. Continuous occurrences of negativities in a person's life, family, or business.
5. Sudden premature death.
6. Patterns of evil occurring at certain designated times or moments.
7. Sudden mishaps such as sickness, car accidents, inexplicable mysteries, etc.

MY INSIGHTS FROM MATTHEW 26:36-46

If care is not taken, any Christian can sleep the sleep of death, no matter the level of spirituality. There are examples cited in this book of the high caliber of people of God who slept the sleep of death, and it brought damaging effects on them and their families. For example, in my opinion, the physical sleep of the disciples of Jesus in the Garden of Gethsemane was a sleep of death. The story can be found in Matthew 26:36-46 (NIV).

> *"36 Then Jesus went with his disciples to a place called Gethsemane, and he said to them, "Sit here while I go over there and pray." 37 He took Peter and the two sons of Zebedee along with him, and he began to be sorrowful and troubled. 38 Then he said to them, "My soul is overwhelmed with sorrow to the point of death. Stay here and keep watch with me."*
>
> *39 Going a little farther, he fell with his face to the ground and prayed, "My Father, if it is possible, may this cup be taken from me. Yet not as I will, but as you will." 40 Then he returned to his disciples and found them sleeping. "Couldn't you men keep watch with me for one hour?" he asked Peter. 41 "Watch*

and pray so that you will not fall into temptation. The spirit is willing, but the flesh is weak." ⁴²He went away a second time and prayed, "My Father, if it is not possible for this cup to be taken away unless I drink it, may your will be done."

*⁴³ When he came back, **he again found them sleeping, because their eyes were heavy**. ⁴⁴ So he left them and went away once more and prayed the third time, saying the same thing. ⁴⁵ Then he returned to the disciples and said to them, "**Are you still sleeping and resting?** Look, the hour has come, and the Son of Man is delivered into the hands of sinners. ⁴⁶ Rise! Let us go! Here comes my betrayer!"*

1. All the disciples experienced the sleep of death.

The first group of the disciples, who were left behind at the initial point of separation, slept the sleep of death. In verse 36, "*³⁶ Then Jesus went with his disciples to a place called Gethsemane, and he said to them, "Sit here while I go over there and pray."*

Here, Jesus told them to sit while He took three out of His disciples to a higher dimension to pray. Why couldn't any of them request to go and pray with Jesus and ask, according to Matthew 7:7? Those who ask are bound to receive. It was when Peter requested from Jesus in Matthew 14:28, *"Command me to come,"* that he was able to walk on water. These disciples slept the sleep of death by not being mindful of Jesus' Words and being sensitive to the happenings around them. They probably ignored what Jesus said.

Before you declare the prayer points the Holy Spirit laid in my spirit, permit me to share the story of a young lady:

A young married lady was invited to a function along with her husband. The young lady informed both her biological mother and mentor that she had a red flag - a bad feeling, an unease in her spirit about attending the function. In other words, she did not feel like going to the occasion. This young lady told her husband who insisted that she must come with him. The husband of this lady even reported his wife to her biological mother and mentor.

The mother of the lady said she also had an uneasy feeling and was skeptical that her daughter should not attend the occasion. Still, she also did not want a situation whereby her daughter and her daughter's husband would be at loggerheads. This dear mother admonished her daughter to proceed with attending the occasion. The young lady attended this occasion with her husband. Unfortunately, this dynamic, beautiful young lady suddenly died a few days after she attended this dreadful occasion with her husband!

The lady confided in her loved ones that some food was given to herself and her husband. She said she knew immediately after she ate the food that she was in trouble. Needless to say, she fell ill immediately. The doctors ran all kinds of tests, but nothing was found wrong with her, and all the medical tests done on her came back perfect. She, however, died, and the autopsy disclosed that it was like she drank cyanide (a chemical solution) and that all her internal organs were shredded into little tiny pieces!

This was an unfortunate story, but I wanted to share it with you to show that insensitivity to the promptings of the Holy Spirit and disregarding personal spiritual feelings can lead to the sleep of death! The truth is that there is no medical test that can diagnose or decode spiritual attacks and satanic arrows unless someone's eyes are opened to the spirit realm. You cannot scientifically diagnose illnesses and spiritual attacks that are satanically generated. The MRI machines, X-ray machines, and blood tests will just turn a patient who is spiritually attacked into an experimental trial-and-error body. Various medical tests will be carried out, but there will be no logical scientific explanations for the person's state of health. Only the power of God can break and destroy satanically-generated sicknesses and spiritual attacks.

The young lady's case described above is a typical example of someone who slept the sleep of death. Firstly, God warned her about the impending danger by giving her uneasy feelings about the occasion. However, she was not the only one who slept the sleep of death. Her insistent husband also did so by insisting that she should attend the occasion which eventually led to her demise. He was not in the Spirit and did not even pick it on the spiritual radar that the occasion should have been avoided. Additionally, her mother should have insisted and advised her to obey her instincts, especially since the mother also felt her daughter should not have gone.

My honest advice is this: not every invitation you receive must be honored. Please do not get me wrong by spiritualizing every event you are invited to. As children of God, we must all learn to tune into the frequency of the Holy Spirit daily. He is our helper in life, and He will guide us in where to go - and where not to go.

2. The disciples (Peter, James, and John) that followed Jesus, according to the Bible passage we are considering, also engaged in the sleep of death.

Jesus selected these three disciples **out of all** His disciples to watch and pray with Him. So, let us analyze together how these three disciples slept the sleep of death, even when they were with Jesus.

- They did not **pay attention** to know Jesus was sorrowful and troubled! These three disciples walked with Jesus for years. Jesus had never been seen like this by them, and they **missed Jesus' moment** of needing their help by being spiritually insensitive or sleeping the sleep of death at the moment of need of their Master.

- Jesus verbally expressed His personal feelings and mental agonies to these three disciples. Jesus said, *"My soul is overwhelmed with sorrow to the point of death. Stay here and keep watch with me."*

Wow! What a difficult time that must have been for our Savior! The people who should have watched with Him slept the sleep of death. I pray for you that those who should watch your back will not ignorantly or deliberately stab your back. Your friends and families, who should keep you in their prayers, will not be "fanned" to sleep by the enemy.

- These three disciples of Christ slept the sleep of death, not only by missing Jesus' feelings and

Words but also by not observing what Jesus verbally **told the disciples to do**. Jesus said, *"Keep watch with me."* They did not watch with Jesus; they slept when they were told to watch! One can even define the sleep of death from this occurrence as **sleeping when you are supposed to be watching.**

- The trio, Peter, James, and John, engaged in the sleep of death not once in this passage but three times! Jesus found these beloved disciples sleeping **three times** when they were supposed to be praying. They slept on duty. May we not sleep on duty in Jesus' name.

In my opinion, **the devil must have fanned them to sleep.** How could the three of them sleep through the ordeal of Jesus in the garden? Even if one or two dozed off, should there not be at least one that could have stayed awake and watched with Christ? This "evil sleep" was not an ordinary natural sleep from body tiredness or fatigue. There must have been **a demonic compulsion and evil assignment to demonize them to sleep at this very crucial hour!**

The Bible says in verse 43, "When he came back, **he again found them sleeping, because their eyes were heavy."** Jesus had a heavy heart, but the disciples had heavy eyes. The devil must have put a spell on them.

The devil does not want any of us to pray, and there is nothing he loves more than putting Christians to sleep when they are supposed to be praying. I pray that you will not sleep the sleep of death at crucial moments in the lives of your loved ones in Jesus' name. Your loved ones, too, will not be fanned to evil sleep when you need them to pray for you. Our eyes will not be heavy with sleep when our hearts should be heavy with prayers in Jesus' Name. Amen!

THE CONSEQUENCES OF THE DISCIPLES' SLEEP OF DEATH

The aftermath of these disciples' sleep of death resulted in many negative things. We should learn from this story so that we and our loved ones will not suffer the wrong consequences. Let's discuss some negative things that happened as a result of the disciples' sleep of death.

1. Wrong Response

When people experience the sleep of death, they are bound to respond negatively to events of life, like the disciples did. In the story of Matthew Chapter 26, especially verse 51 (NIV), *"⁵¹ With that, one of Jesus' companions reached for his sword, drew it out and struck the servant of the high priest, cutting off his ear."* Bible scholars have referred to this companion as Peter. So, Peter was quick to **respond wrongly** because, just before this occurrence, he **slept when he was supposed to have prayed**.

The other disciples' responses, or lack thereof, were also wrong moves. They were also in the garden **and did nothing** or were too dumbfounded because **they never knew Jesus would be attacked despite Jesus' direct and indirect teachings about His death!**

Conclusively, all the disciples responded wrongly due to sleeping the sleep of death. Peter's wrong response was of the flesh. A lack of prayer will make any Christian act in the flesh. Acting in the flesh means your actions or reactions are engineered by how you feel instead of how the Holy Spirit leads.

2. The Denial of Jesus

The disciples denied Jesus in many ways. After the scenario that happened in the garden, Peter verbally denied Jesus three times (Luke 22:54-62). Likewise, there are many strange ways Christians are indirectly denying Jesus today. Such denials happen because people are **carelessly sleeping the sleep of death** without being aware.

3. Waste of Investment

These three disciples wasted Jesus' investments in their lives. Remember, Jesus had other disciples, but this trio

(Peter, James, and John) are the people I would call *"Jesus' inner caucus."* **These three disciples were privileged and chosen out of the other disciples to go higher with Jesus.** There were places Jesus went to without the other disciples, except these three! Jesus invested more in them than the others. According to Luke 12:48 (NKJV), *"To whom much is given, from him much will be required."* Yet when Jesus' investments in these three were supposed to yield dividends and good results, they were nowhere to be found.

The Bible says in Matthew 26:56b (NIV), *"Then all the disciples deserted him and fled."* Jesus' "inner caucus" was part of those who ran and left Jesus during His trial! Who would have believed this would happen? All the disciples fled because they all slept the sleep of death through insensitivity. The three disciples slept the sleep of death physically and spiritually and engaged in the sleep of death through insensitivity. If the three disciples had prayed, it might have helped them and the "left behind" disciples to avoid all the blunders they committed. Yes! Jesus would still have died, but they could have eased things for themselves and set good examples for us.

God has invested a lot in all of us, and I pray that we will yield good dividends for God in Jesus' name. None of us will invest in the wrong people. Our families, businesses, friends, and "inner caucuses" shall be good investments.

I pray for you, dear reader; those who should fight for you will not be found wanting; they will measure up. Those who should fight for you will not desert you or fight with you; they will not fight against you. They will not experience the sleep of death like Judas and will not deflect to your enemies to fight against you in the name of Jesus.

4. Future Attack

As a result of the disciples' sleep of death, the devil was able to attack their future. Things could have been worse for all the disciples, especially Peter, because according to Luke 22:31, Jesus warned Peter, "Peter, the devil has taken permission to sift you like wheat, but I have prayed for you." What an attribute of a great leader who is sensitive! Though the disciples did not pray, Jesus prayed.

I pray for you that your future is secured in the hollow of God's palm (Isaiah 49:16). You are inscribed in God's hands. **The devil and evil people will not attack your present or tamper with your future and the future of your loved ones in Jesus' name!**

Dear reader, I have two assignments for you! Firstly, did you notice that some words or sentences were italicized? If you did, give yourself a pat on the back because it shows that you are sensitive or becoming sensitive to the things you are seeing and reading, as well as the things around you.

So, here goes my assignment.

Kindly take the time to formulate your prayer points using the words or sentences in bold lettering. You may even pick more words or sentences for prayers apart from the ones written above. Also, join me in declaring the prayers in Chapter 12 for yourself, your career, your business, and your loved ones. Always remember to tweak the prayers so you do not have to say them verbatim.

CHAPTER FOUR

The Prostitute and Her Sleep of Death

There was a careless prostitute who engaged in the sleep of death in the Bible. This story can be found in 1 Kings Chapter 3. It was the story of this prostitute that the Lord used in giving me this revelation on the sleep of death.

I have been a Christian for many years, and I have never heard or read the story in this chapter the way the Holy Spirit explained it to me. Many Sunday school teachers taught me the story of the prostitute, but the lesson emphasized through the story was to show the wisdom God gave Solomon. I have also read and preached about the story, but it was to show the level of wisdom

Solomon operated in. As a young elementary student, I have seen the story dramatized in diverse ways, but nobody taught or spoke about the sleep of death.

All my teachers were correct! The story was essentially about the wisdom God gave Solomon, and how he put this wisdom to work and was able to resolve the problem between the two prostitutes in the story. However, God opened my eyes to see that the story was not only about the wisdom He gave Solomon. I will explain it in this chapter.

Many years ago, God taught me to pray this prayer before sleeping: *Lord, as I sleep right now, help me that my spirit will not be asleep (this means that as I sleep, my spirit will not be weak, submissive, and permissive to all kinds of spirits). Lord, please make my spirit aggressive, dangerous, and destructive against the kingdom of darkness in Jesus' name.*

I have prayed the prayer above for many years, and then the Holy Spirit led me to the story in 1 Kings Chapter 3. The Holy Spirit said, "One way for a person not to sleep the sleep of death is **for the person's spirit to be alert while the body is deep in sleep.**" Then, I got the revelation of how the prostitute in the book of 1 Kings 3:16-21 slept the sleep of death.

Let's consider the story in 1 Kings 3:16-21 (AMP).

> "*16 Then two women who were prostitutes came to the king and stood before him. 17 And the one woman said, "O my lord, this woman and I live in the same house; and I gave birth to a child while she was in the house. 18 And on the third day after I gave birth, this woman also gave birth. And we were [alone] together; no one else was with us in the house, just we two.*
>
> *19 Now this woman's son died during the night, because she lay on him [and smothered him]. 20 So she got up in the middle of the night and took my son from [his place] beside me while your maidservant was asleep, and laid him on her bosom, and laid her dead son on my bosom. 21 When I got up in the morning to nurse my son, behold, he was dead. But when I examined him carefully in the morning, behold, it was not my son, the one whom I had borne."*

Let us highlight some of the things that showed that this woman slept the sleep of death: The two women in the passage could be differentiated as the one who slept the sleep of death and the one who did evil exchange (the latter being the one who switched a dead child for the living one).

SPIRITUAL SLUMBER

1. The prostitute slept the sleep of death by being oblivious to the evil happening around her. The two prostitutes both gave birth to sons; one was three days older than the other. To be specific, the son of the woman who slept the sleep of death was three days older than the son of the one who did evil. They slept together, though we are not sure whether they slept on the same mat together or in different rooms. The woman who did evil switched her dead baby for the living baby from the woman who slept the sleep of death. The woman who slept the sleep of death was so sound asleep, that her newborn baby was carried away from her, and she did not notice! She slept through the switching operation! How long did the switching take? We are not aware, but this woman slept through it all!

2. This woman slept the sleep of death all night long. The woman who slept the sleep of death was so deep in sleep while the dead baby was laid on her bosom. The weight of the dead baby was placed on her bosom, not beside her, and she still slept through it all. What a careless sleep! Whichever way you think the baby was placed, there is a womanly instinct that should have picked the heaviness taking place around this woman. Whenever a newborn is in a family, there is often an adult, either the biological parents or the caregivers, who keep checking to see if

the baby is alive and breathing. This was not the case with this woman who slept the sleep of death in this story; she slept all night long!

3. The prostitute slept the sleep of death while her son was stolen and his destiny was swapped for a dead destiny. This woman who slept the sleep of death, in my opinion, judged her carelessness by the words of her mouth. She said in verse 21, *"21 When I got up in the morning to nurse my son, behold, he was dead."* How could she have slept all night long, and she had a nursing baby with her? There was no helper for both women. She knew nobody was there to help her nurse the baby at night, to change soiled clothes, yet she never woke up to check on her baby! She was sound asleep while the destiny of her son was swapped, and the baby was physically stolen.

4. This woman who slept the sleep of death further showed her carelessness and insensitivity as she went further to explain the occurrence to King Solomon in verse 21: *"21 When I got up in the morning to nurse my son, behold, he was dead. But when I examined him carefully in the morning, behold, it was not my son, the one whom I had borne."*

Follow with me carefully to digest what this lady said. In verse 21, she noticed that her son was dead. She only found out her son was dead when she held the dead **baby in her arms and was about to breastfeed him!** This woman was going to nurse a dead baby that was not her baby! This lady was not going to breastfeed at night but in the morning! Note that death and life are in the power of the tongue (Proverbs 18:21), so be sensitive!

Mind your words. The dead baby was not her son. Her words could be sensitively, correctly, and spiritually worded as when she got up to feed her baby, she found out that the **dead baby she picked to feed was the other prostitute's baby. Her baby was not dead but was alive.** Honestly, I am not being over-reactive with the words we speak. The Lord warns us about negative words, dead words, and idle words.

5. The prostitute who experienced the sleep of death said that it was through careful examination in broad daylight that she discovered that the dead baby was not her son. **The progression of the carelessness of this lady's sleep of death** may be seen as itemized below:

She was fast asleep when the evil switcher:

- Took her baby from beside her.
- Carried the living baby and repositioned the living baby to her bed.

- Brought her dead son and placed it not on the side, but on top of the careless prostitute's chest. Carrying a dead weight on her chest and for how long? And yet, she did not wake up!

- The careless prostitute did not wake up through the night to check on or even nurse her baby.

- She eventually woke up in the morning, **but** it took her some time to examine the dead child before she knew the dead child was not her child! I am positive **that this lady, being a prostitute, would not need a long time to figure out what clothes, shoes, and other apparel she would need for her trade of prostitution**. Still, it took her some time and a thorough examination to notice the dead child was not her child.

The points highlighted above showed that this woman slept the sleep of death. This is very typical of those who sleep this type of death. Many things would be violated in their dreams, and such people would still be blind or oblivious to the negative things and the evil power sources that cause bad things to them. Sometimes, the victims of the sleep of death are the enemies of their households, friends, or people they are intimately engaged with. Also, the very ones vandalizing their lives and destinies are the ones as close to them as teeth are as close to the mouth. It's just like the meaning of an adage in my dialect, which says, "The insects destroying vegetables and fruits are not insects from outside the fruits and vegetables. The vegetable destroyers are the insects feeding and living on and with the vegetables."

Once again, I must sound a cautionary note here; I am not an author of gloom and doom, inciting families against families and friends against friends. I am a people-lover and would go all the way for my family. The point I am promoting is spiritual alertness and mental sensitivity to the events of our lives.

PRAYER FOR YOURSELF:

Lord, help me to be spiritually alert and mentally sensitive to the events of life around me. My eyes are anointed to see beyond the natural. My ears are quickened, and I will not be spiritually dull in hearing.

ADDITIONAL INSIGHTS FROM THE STORY OF THE PROSTITUTES

1. The Wisdom of Solomon to Correctly Decode the Rightful Mother of The Child

Certainly, the lady who slept the sleep of death thanked Jehovah after King Solomon's verdict. She must have appreciated the Lord for the depth of wisdom given to Solomon by God. This woman, who slept the sleep of death, was able to take her living son back through the wisdom of Solomon. An unwise king or judge would have destroyed the destiny of that child. The king or judge could have ordered the child to live with another family until the case was resolved. The king or judge could have given the child to the wrong mother, who would not have raised the child according to purpose.

Do you know how many destinies have been tampered with, switched around, vandalized, destroyed, and possibly killed due to self, parental, or caregivers' carelessness and sleep of death?

2. The Other Prostitute, the "Evil Swapper," in a Way, Also Slept the Sleep of Death

I guess you are surprised about this. I will mention three points about the second prostitute, and you can ask the Holy Spirit to teach and give you prayer points from the life of these two ladies. In the story, 1 Kings 3:19 (AMP) says, *"19 Now this woman's son died during the night, because she lay on him [and smothered him]."*

Firstly, I observed that she laid on her son and smothered him.

Please note that a son in this story can be related to:
- Career
- Marriage

- Destiny
- Business
- Relationship
- Health
- Finances, etc.

A son, here, can be anything connected directly or indirectly to a person, a destiny, or a family. We were told that the son, in this case, died because the mother smothered him! I am sure this lady would not have wanted this child to die. The child's death was an accidental death, or maybe, due to a nonchalant attitude, that is, the sleep of death of the mother. I pray we will not directly or indirectly kill the good things in our lives.

Secondly, I observed the great extent to which the lady went to actualize her evil acts! She was so careless to have slept on her baby and was so crafty and witty in quickly putting evil plans together. There are people like her who do not know how to do good but are quick and very calculated in doing evil!

Thirdly, my observation, as given by the Holy Ghost, is the mystery of two prostitutes in the same place, the same house by themselves (verse 18). Was it the custom for prostitutes to live together? I do not believe so. Rahab, in the book of Joshua, Chapter 2, lived by herself on the wall of the city. Were these prostitutes together because they shared the same fate or because they were going through the same challenges? Were they friends? Why were they living together? Did they plan to be pregnant around the same time? There are many questions surrounding the mystery of these two prostitutes living together. It is a sleep of death to hang around only those whose lives can benefit your purpose in life.

Have you heard of these adages: "Birds of a feather flock together," and "Show me your friends, and I will tell you who you are or will become." This implies that your association with people can either make or mar you. The Bible also says, *"Evil communications corrupt good manners"* (1 Corinthians 15:33, KJV).

This prostitute smothered her son. There are many ways people can smother other people in their lives. There is the testimony of a father who switched the glories of the destinies of his daughters just so he could live as a rich man.

During one of the crusades organized by our ministry outside of the United States, we met a Christian lady who told us about the ordeal of her father's children. All of these children, about six of them, were professionals who had a great education. However, none of them passed the professional examinations needed to become licensed professionals in their various fields of endeavor. The mother of these six siblings knew something was wrong. She told her children that something was wrong but she could not put her finger on what could be the root-causing problems in her children's lives. The father of these siblings was a very rich man. However, he suddenly died mysteriously, and it was understood that he was in a cultic and fetish fraternity.

Would you permit me to subjectively conclude that this dear mother also slept the sleep of death? How could you be married to such a man, and you never suspected that he or someone connected to the husband was the cause of her children's dilemma?

At the crusade ground, Dr. Festus Adeyeye, my husband and the crusader, prayed with one of the daughters. This lady was already slated to repeat the same professional exam for the sixth time. The man of God told her God would help her; that anointing had destroyed the yoke of her life. The lady contacted us later and informed us that God came through for her - she passed her professional exam. She got her long-awaited breakthrough — what a great joy!

The lady shared the testimony that shortly after the prayer, many things unfolded, and the secret of the evil behind the failures in her family was revealed! The mother of this dear lady suddenly saw a strange-looking piece of paper on which the names of her six daughters and some incantations about their futures were written in their father's handwriting. The incantations detailed that the man's six daughters would all be educated to the degree levels but would not secure any meaningful jobs with their degrees! It was also detailed that he, the father, had diabolically switched the future glories of his children for him to be rich and be a person of affluence! He smothered the future glories of all his daughters just so he could be rich; what a wicked father!

When people sleep the sleep of death, their destinies can be vandalized, switched, covered, or stolen, just as this man stole the destinies of his daughters.

I also had to examine my life when I understood that people could be alive and sleep the sleep of death daily. Dear reader, do you need to reflect also? Are there things looking awkwardly strange happening in your life or family? If you are married, have you checked negative trends in the family you are married into? Are there breakthroughs that have been prolonged and is everybody placing natural answers to delays in breakthroughs?

Do you know that another way Satan "fans" people to experience the sleep of death is when people intellectualize or naturalize spiritual happenings or events? I pray that the Spirit of the Almighty God will open your eyes to understanding and that you will not be insensitive to spiritual matters, in Jesus' name.

Some prayer points can be drawn from the five people in the story of 1 Kings Chapter 3.

1. The baby whose destiny was smothered upon and killed while resting.

2. The baby who was alive and whose real mother had to be determined. This baby's destiny faced controversy as it was swapped and stolen.

3. The careless prostitute who slept the sleep of death.

4. The evil switcher who destroyed her child and was ready to damage and destroy another family.

5. The wise King, Solomon, who was endowed with wisdom by God.

You will find detailed prayer points on the above in Section Four of Chapter Twelve. I pray the Holy Spirit will enable and empower you to formulate and custom-make other prayers to fit your situations.

The babies in the story can represent anything good in life; remember, children are gifts from the Lord. Good things such as babies, businesses, marriages, health, careers, ideas, relationships, families, different projects, the bright future, etc.

CHAPTER FIVE

Deliverer Demoted to a Grinder of Grains

Another personality in the Bible who experienced the sleep of death was Samson. Samson's case was very pathetic. He slept the sleep of death and became a grinder of grains and an object of amusement in the hands of his enemies. He is a classic example of how people should not play with their destinies, no matter the prophetic declaration released upon their lives.

Samson was born to lead the Israelites as a judge and to destroy their lifelong enemy — the Philistines. There were angelic visitations and instructions not one time, but two times before Samson was even conceived by his parents. You would think such validation of Samson's destiny and future was sealed permanently. Well, as far as God was concerned, that validation was sealed, but just because God's plan is prophesied and announced does not mean it will automatically come to pass without being tested, tried, and thwarted by Satan. This is one of the reasons why every child of God must pray not to sleep the sleep of death, but to incubate and deliver one's prophetic destiny through prayer and sometimes, fasting. Every prophecy given must be conceived, barricaded, and delivered through spiritual exercises of faith, fasting, and prayer.

Like Samson, who played with the prophecy of his destiny, my General Overseer, Dr. Festus, shared the story of two brothers whose destinies were foretold while they were young. The younger was told he would be the king of the village, while the older was told he would be a nuisance in the same village. The younger brother never did anything with his life, and everyone in the town knew he would be the future king and leader. He was addressed and referred to as the future king of the village. The older brother had a vision. He worked on himself and even left his town of birth and resided in another town. Afterward, this older brother became a big-time farmer and was well-known and respected in the town he lived in.

Not too long ago, there was famine in his village of

birth, and it was so bad that people started migrating to other places. This older brother was discovered and recognized by one of the immigrants from his village of birth. As soon as he was recognized by one of his townsmen, the news of this older brother traveled far and fast back into his village of birth. The leaders from his village of birth went to him and begged him to be their king and rule over them since he was now a very successful farmer. This older brother relocated to his hometown and became the king. Needless to say, the younger brother never made anything out of his life because he felt there was a prophecy over his life, and he never took concrete steps to actualize the prophecy.

One important lesson from this story is to work hard, work smart on your goals, and take concrete and appropriate steps in fulfilling your plans. The promises of God in the Bible are prophesied over every child of God. However, every prophecy does not automatically come to pass; it must be birthed with prayer and watched with carefulness and spiritual sensitivity. Apostle Paul told Timothy in the book of 1 Timothy 1:18 (NIV), *"18 Timothy, my son, I am giving you this command in keeping with the prophecies once made about you, so that by recalling them you may fight the battle well."* No matter the words that might have been said about your life, you must choose not to live carelessly.

Samson can be likened to the younger brother in the story above, who played with his destiny and the prophecy of God in his life. In my opinion, Samson engaged in the mental, physical, and spiritual sleep of death. Let's look at a few things he did to buttress my point about his sleep of death.

THE MENTAL, PHYSICAL, AND SPIRITUAL SLEEP OF DEATH EXPERIENCED BY SAMSON

Firstly, it was plain disobedience and dishonor to God that Samson married Delilah. Samson knew better than to marry from uncircumcised Philistines. There was no recording of any prophecy or angelic visitation to David's parents before David's birth. Yet, he knew that there was a clear distinction between those who served God in his generation and those who did not. David did not mince words; he identified Goliath for who he was—an uncircumcised Philistine (1 Samuel 17:26).

The Israelites were raised from birth to know they were different, and even the Scriptures warned them not to intermarry with any Gentiles (Deuteronomy 7:3). In my opinion, it is the sleep of death not to follow instructions written in the Scriptures. Samson was raised to destroy the Philistines and not to marry any of them. The Bible says, "If you inter-marry, they will turn your hearts away from the living God" (Deuteronomy 7:3-4).

Then, how did Samson sleep the sleep of death?

Secondly, I believe Samson played games with his destiny and slept all kinds of death—spiritually (by not paying attention to his surroundings). Samson was not spiritually sensitive, according to the story in Judges 16:4-20. He was playing with what God gave him as his source of uniqueness and purpose. The wife wanted to know the source of his secret — this is not what you play and joke around with. This was what defined Samson's reason for living — his purpose.

Thirdly, Samson fell into a deep sleep physically, so he was not conscious when the strand of his hair was cut. Oh, what a sleep!

CHAPTER SIX

David Versus the Killer in King's Clothing

King David came on the scene of the Bible when God introduced him through Prophet Samuel as a "man after his own heart", according to 1 Samuel 13:14 (NIV) which says, *"14 But now your kingdom will not endure;* the LORD has sought out a man after his own heart **and appointed him ruler of his people,** *because you have not kept the LORD's command"* and Acts 13:22 (NIV) which says, *"22 After removing Saul, he made David their king. God testified concerning him: 'I have found David son of Jesse, a man after my own heart; he will do everything I want him to do.'"*

God appointed David to be king after Saul had disobeyed

SPIRITUAL SLUMBER

God. Many things can be written about David, such as he was a warrior, praise leader, God-lover, poet, king, and other wonderful things. I, however, want to bring our attention to how David did not sleep the sleep of death. Though he was anointed king of Israel, it looked increasingly difficult for this promise of God to come to pass in his life. This was because the first king of Israel, Saul (the predecessor of David), wanted David dead out of his jealousy against him. David, however, escaped all the traps of death set against him by Saul.

Can you imagine the odds of escaping death when the most powerful man in the world was looking to kill him? David escaped all the death traps because God helped him and he was also spiritually sensitive to the things happening around him.

Let's discuss how David was able to escape all these forms of death:

1. Saul, the killer in a king's clothing, threw spears at David more than two times, according to 1 Samuel 18:10-11. While David was playing the instrument before Saul, he was alert spiritually and was able to sense the evil intentions that Saul had towards him. People may be around you doing good things outwardly, like Saul was outwardly prophesying, but inwardly, killing David. Saul said in his heart in verse 11 (NIV), *"11 and he hurled it, saying to himself, "I'll*

pin David to the wall." That night, David made good his escape. In these three instances, David escaped what I called "arrows of death."

2. David escaped Saul's secret evil plot by using secondary killers. David escaped the assignment of death. According to 1 Samuel 18:22 & 25, Saul tried to use the Philistines to carry out his plot to kill David. He sent his attendant to David with a disguised death plot. Saul sent people to talk David into becoming the son-in-law of the king. Saul planned to have David fall by the hands of the Philistines. However, David thought he would become Saul's in-law, so he went and killed not a hundred Philistines but doubled the number and killed two hundred Philistines. Again, God's hands of protection were strong on David's life, and he escaped this evil death from the killer king.

3. David escaped the bed of death (1 Samuel 19:13-17, AMP).

> *"13 And Michal took the household idol and laid it on the bed, put a pillow of goats' hair at its head, and covered it with clothes. 14 And when Saul sent messengers to take David, she said, "He is sick." 15 Then Saul sent the messengers [again] to see David, saying, "Bring him up to me on his*

> bed [if necessary], so that I may kill him." *16* When the messengers came in, there was the household idol on the bed with a quilt of goats' hair at its head. *17* Saul said to Michal, "Why have you deceived me like this and let my enemy go, so that he has escaped?" Michal answered Saul, "He said to me, 'Let me go! Why should I kill you?'"

Saul's daughter (Michal), who was given to David as a trap to kill David (1 Samuel 18:21), was the one who helped David escape the bed of death. It is my prayer for you that your enemy's daughter will be a solution instead of a problem for you. May your enemy's families be helpers of destiny to protect you in Jesus' name.

4. David escaped the seat of death (1 Samuel 20:25-31).

> "*18* Then Jonathan said to David, "Tomorrow is the New Moon [festival], and you will be missed because your seat will be empty." (1 Samuel 20:18, AMP)

Saul expected David to dine at the royal palace with him during the new moon festival, and he intended to kill David. In 1 Samuel 20:5-8 (NIV), it was obvious that David did not sleep the sleep of death. He was well aware of who his enemy was and correctly interpreted

Saul's actions.

> *⁵ So David said, "Look, tomorrow is the New Moon feast, and I am supposed to dine with the king; but let me go and hide in the field until the evening of the day after tomorrow. ⁶ If your father misses me at all, tell him, 'David earnestly asked my permission to hurry to Bethlehem, his hometown, because an annual sacrifice is being made there for his whole clan.'*
>
> *⁷ If he says, 'Very well,' then your servant is safe. But if he loses his temper, you can be sure that he is determined to harm me. ⁸ As for you, show kindness to your servant, for you have brought him into a covenant with you before the LORD. If I am guilty, then kill me yourself! Why hand me over to your father?"*

Just as David correctly predicted, Saul flared up at David's absence. In fact, God was so angry that he tried to kill his son, Jonathan (1 Samuel 20). As a result of this, David's chair was empty two days in a row.

5. David escaped the city of death (1 Samuel 23). David took his men to Keilah to fight the Philistines. In fact, David's men were afraid to follow him because

of Saul. David, being a man after God's heart, inquired of the Lord if he should go to Keilah. God told David twice to go to this town.

> *⁷ Saul was told that David had gone to Keilah, and he said, "God has delivered him into my hands, for David has imprisoned himself by entering a town with gates and bars." ⁸ **And Saul called up all his forces for battle,** to go down to Keilah to besiege David and his men."*

Children of God should know that just because God authorizes a place, a job, or an assignment does not mean challenges will be absent. Two times, God assured David to fight at Keilah. David was told Saul was coming there with all the forces of Israel to kill David. Guess what? God even told David that the people of Keilah, whom David went to help, would surrender David to Saul! The Bible says that David and his men left Keilah at once. God did not give David into the hands of Saul.

6. David escaped the informants of death. About seven times, there were instances that people were informing Saul about David's movements. I call such people "evil informants."

According to 1 Samuel 23:19 (AMP), *"¹⁹ Then the **Ziphites came to Saul** at Gibeah, saying, "Is David* *not hiding with us in strongholds of Horesh, on the hill of Hachilah, which is south of [b]Jeshimon?"* Saul almost caught up with David, when he heard that David was in the Wilderness of Maon. Then, Saul made another move according to 1 Samuel 23:26-28 (AMP), *"²⁶ Saul went on one side of the mountain, and David and his men on the other side of the mountain. And David was hurrying to get away from Saul, for Saul and his men were surrounding David and his men to capture them. ²⁷ **But** a messenger came to Saul, saying, "Hurry and come, because the Philistines have attacked the land." ²⁸ So Saul returned from pursuing David and went to meet the Philistines; therefore they called that place the Rock of Escape."*

At this point, Saul and his men had already cornered David and his men. The former group was rounding the latter; there was no more escape! However, God showed up for David just before the bottom would fall off, and God raised an evil report for Saul in 1 Samuel 23:27-28. Wow, I could almost perceive David wiping out the sweat of fear away from his forehead. God came through for him at the nick of time, just before his archenemy could catch him! David called the place "the Rock of Escape." Right now, Jesus should be your Rock of Escape because, with Him, you will be spiritually alert to escape all traps and forms of death.

CHAPTER SEVEN

Parents, Reject the Sleep of Death!

I believe good parents are proactive when it comes to barricading the destinies and the future of their children. However, despite their proactiveness, a parent may still be spiritually insensitive and unaware of the devices of Satan. Spiritual insensitivity is a big door the enemy uses to mess up the glorious plans of God for children.

The woman, who is the major actress in the main text of this book, according to 1 Kings Chapter 3, slept the sleep of death. As a matter of fact, both prostitutes engaged in the sleep of death. The prostitute who slept through the night while her baby was switched was, in my opinion, too lazy, careless, natural, and insensitive to her surroundings. The culprit that switched the baby also slept the sleep of death. The two women represent two kinds of mothers, and I will explain further.

The prostitute, whose child was switched, represents the kinds of women who are aware of the good things God has given them, but they can become spiritually asleep till those good things are lost. The good things could be marriage, children, careers, businesses, other relationships, etc.

A practical example that came to my mind was the story of a lady I met in Europe who was married to an unbeliever. The couple was unable to have children, and during their waiting, this lady met a high school friend in their town of residence. This friend had just relocated to the town and she was looking to move to a different apartment from where she was at the time, so they reconnected. This high school friend was also an unbeliever, and the naive Christian lady brought her unbelieving friend to live in one room in the house bought by herself and her husband. To cut the preambles of this story, this unbelieving friend became pregnant, and you guessed correctly, the baby's father was the Christian lady's husband! This dear Christian lady eventually left the marriage and the house for her high school friend and her ex-husband.

While I am not insensitive to the wickedness and evil done to this Christian lady, there is no doubt she slept the sleep of death. Pertinent clarifications will reveal this fact, such as:

- Did she ask the Lord before bringing the lady over?

- Not every good act is God's will, and God said in Proverbs 3:5-6 (AMP), *"5 Trust in and rely confidently on the LORD with all your heart And do not rely on your own insight or understanding. 6 [a] In all your ways know and acknowledge and recognize Him, And He will make your paths straight and smooth [removing obstacles that block your way]."*

- That unbelieving lady was a big obstacle, and God would have removed her only if the Christian lady had prayed.

- My next question to this Christian lady is, "What exactly were you expecting from an unbeliever or two unbelievers?" Did the Bible not say in Matthew 7:18 (NKJV), *"18 A good tree cannot bear bad fruit, nor can a bad tree bear good fruit."* Unbelievers do not have the Holy Spirit inside of them to guide them; they make decisions based on their five senses or what I call the "Adamic nature." This is the nature that pleases self at the expense of others. The nature or personality that gets what you want to get, by all means possible, no matter who gets hurt or trampled, so far, you get what you want.

- How did she bear herself naked to someone she had not met or related to for some years? She might have known this lady while they were in high school, but people do change for many reasons. I love the Scripture in John 2:24 (AMP) that says, *"24 But Jesus, for His part, did not entrust Himself to them, because He knew all people [and understood the [a]superficiality and fickleness of human nature]."* The Message translation of this same verse says, *"But Jesus didn't entrust his life to them. He knew them inside and out, knew how untrustworthy they were."* Jesus knew how untrustworthy the people around Him were.

As parents, you must not be spiritually insensitive. Be alert and watchful; barricade and build a hedge over and around the things God has given to you.

The second prostitute, who laid on her child and smothered the child, represents Christians who do not appreciate the good things in their lives. They don't take care of what they have because they do not know its worth or value. Whatever you do not value, you do not care for or take care of, and what you do not appreciate will depreciate. Such people do not appreciate their spouses if they are married. If they are employees, they do not care for their good jobs or careers God has given them until those things become lost. It does not matter what it is - business, relationships, health, or anything at all; this group of people will sleep the sleep of death until the good things in their lives are lost, killed, or messed up by others.

The Bible says in Proverbs 14:1 (AMP), *"The wise woman builds her house [on a foundation of godly precepts, and her household thrives], But the foolish one [who lacks spiritual insight] tears it down with her own hands [by ignoring godly principles]."*

You may as well insert a person in the Scripture above, instead of a woman for this point. The good things given by God are torn down and lost through negative comments, grumbling, complaining, comparison, lack of interest, uncooperative attitude, ingratitude, lack of patience, and failure to apply godly principles, and such character will "smother the good things" we have, like the prostitute who smothered her baby.

These kinds of people also do not care for the good things that other people have. Somebody who does not care about what he or she has, will also not care for the things owned by others. There is an African adage that says, "When someone has messed up her clothes, he or she will not care to tear another person's clothes." This was true in the case of this prostitute who already killed her baby through the sleep of death, no wonder she wanted the living baby to be killed also.

Truthfully, when both prostitutes were arguing and claiming the only living child, and there was no third party or any witness, how would anyone know the true mother of the living baby? How do you administer justice in a case like this? Look at the wisdom of God displayed by King Solomon in 1 Kings 3:24 -27 (AMP), *"*^{24} *Then the king said, "Bring me a sword." So, they brought a sword before the king.* ^{25} *Then the king said, "Cut the living child in two, and give half to the one [woman] and half to the other."* ^{26} *Then the woman whose child was the living one spoke to the king, for she was deeply moved over her son, "O my lord, give her the living child, and by no means kill him." But the other said, "He shall be neither mine nor yours; cut him!* ^{27} *Then the king said, "Give the first woman [who is pleading for his life] the living child, and by no means kill him. She is his mother."*

Thank God for the wisdom of God displayed by King Solomon; the baby was restored to the right mother. However, this prostitute displayed the wickedness and selfishness of the second group of people who do not value God's gift in their lives. This can be seen by her response in verse 26b, *"But the other said, "He shall be neither mine nor yours; cut him!"* She wanted the living baby cut into two. When people have messed up their clothes, they will not mind cutting yours! Be very sensitive and alert; do not sleep the sleep of death in all areas of your life.

I remember the true story of a brother who was processing his travels abroad from Africa. The brother was in his early 40s at the time of this process. He went to seek advice from his older stepbrother; he wanted to know if it was a good idea to leave his country to relocate to the United Kingdom. The older brother discouraged him and mentioned many reasons why it was not a good idea for this brother to relocate at his age. Unfortunately, the younger brother, too, took this advice and never consulted God or other people. The man never traveled, especially based on age, as advised by his older stepbrother.

You may find it hard to believe, but the same older brother relocated to the United Kingdom 20 years after he told his younger brother that relocating in his early 40s was a bad idea. Do not lose your vision or plan based on somebody else's negative experiences. Do not give up on your children, career, or self. There is absolutely nothing difficult for God to turn around.

God can create a road where you need a road and

can block or turn the same road into "a closed or an obstructed way" for your enemies, just like the story of the Egyptian chariots who got drowned in the Red Sea, and God made way for the Israelites. Put your absolute trust in God, His Word, and dependable Christians. God does not want us to experience the sleep of death; it can be devastating and destructive.

BIBLICAL EXAMPLES OF PARENTS WHO SLEPT THE SLEEP OF DEATH

Eli (The Priest)

Eli, the priest, experienced the sleep of death. It's clearly explained in the book of 1 Samuel, Chapters two and three. Eli, in 1 Samuel 2:23-25, gave his disapproval to the act of dishonoring God and the things of God that his children displayed. However, in the verses above, Eli appeared to just frown at what his children did by asking his children the reasons they were acting unruly. Frowning or questioning a bad behavior is different from scolding, rebuking, or even disciplining a bad behavior.

Look at what God said about Eli in 1 Samuel 3:11-13 (AMP), *"11 The LORD said to Samuel, "Behold, I am about to do a thing in Israel at which both ears of everyone who hears it will ring. 12 On that day I will carry out against Eli everything that I have spoken concerning his house (family), from beginning to end.* ¹³ *Now I have told him that I am about to judge his house forever for the sinful behavior which he knew [was happening] because his sons were bringing a curse on themselves [dishonoring and blaspheming God]* **<u>and he did not rebuke them."</u>**

The statement, "And he did not rebuke them," showed that Eli questioned their actions, but he did not rebuke or even discipline them by at least asking them to step down for a short time or suspend them temporarily from the office. Eli was the judge and the high priest over God's people at this time. He could have disciplined his children since he stood in the place of a father, judge, and high priest. However, the soft heart of a father probably took over him. So, instead of administering justice as he should have done, he only expressed his dissatisfaction but did not take a firm stand to effect the right changes in his children. God took this as dishonor to Him. What Eli did was actually to satisfy his children at the expense of honoring God.

This, in this case, was a sleep of death — being insensitive to the things of God and the things around him that can bring devastating effects on his family. The part that even showed that Eli was out of touch with God and the things of God, in my opinion, is in 1 Samuel 2:26-36 and 1 Samuel 3:18. God sent a Prophet and little

Samuel to Eli with a message of the devastations that would happen to his family as a result of his children's behavior and his own inability to rebuke them. His response to God's warning was scary. This is found in verse 18 (AMP), *"¹⁸ So Samuel told him everything, hiding nothing from him. And Eli said, "It is the LORD; may He do what seems good to Him."*

Wow! So this was what Eli would say after working for God all those years. He could not even intercede for his family. Eli knew how merciful and compassionate God was, and he could have asked for mercy, forgiveness, and a reversal of the repercussions; God, in His mercy, would have changed the verdict. Eli slept the sleep of death, and he even "snored" in it.

As parents, you must be careful not to choose your children over God. Parents should be bold in addressing their adult children whenever they are living contrary to the Word. Parents need to be firm in making their stand known, in love, to their adult children. Parents should be ready to do their parts. Let God see that you have not compromised and that you are not dishonoring Him by tolerating ungodliness in the lives of your children.

Remember, the sleep of death is also insensitivity to the things of the Spirit, carelessness, and a nonchalant attitude toward ungodliness or anything that dishonors God. It also refers to being reactive instead of proactive after damages have already been done. What Eli's boys did was very costly, but I believe God took Eli's failure even more seriously because he failed to take the appropriate steps to honor God over his children. Read the repercussions of Eli's sleep of death in 1 Samuel 2:27-36 (AMP).

> *"27 Then a man of God (prophet) came to Eli and said to him, "Thus says the LORD: 'Did I not plainly reveal Myself to the house of your father (ancestor) when they were in Egypt in bondage to Pharaoh's house? 28 Moreover, [a] I selected him out of all the tribes of Israel to be My priest, to go up to My altar, to burn incense, to wear an ephod before Me. And [from then on] I gave to the house of your father all the fire offerings of the sons of Israel.*
>
> *29 Why then do you kick at (despise) My sacrifice and My offering which I commanded in My dwelling place, and honor your sons more than Me, by fattening yourselves with the choicest part of every offering of My people Israel?' 30 Therefore the LORD God*

of Israel declares, 'I did indeed say that your house and that of [Aaron] your father would walk [in priestly service] before Me forever.' But now the LORD declares, 'Far be it from Me—for those who honor Me I will honor, and those who despise Me will be insignificant and contemptible.

³¹ Behold, the time is coming when I will cut off your strength and the strength of your father's house, so that there will not be an old man in your house. ³² You will look at the distress of My [b]house (the tabernacle), in spite of all the good which God will do for Israel, and there will never again be an old man in your house.

³³ Yet I will not cut off every man of yours from My altar; your eyes will fail from weeping and your soul will grieve, and all those born in your house will die as men [in the prime of life]. ³⁴ This will be the sign to you which shall come concerning your two sons, Hophni and Phinehas: on the same day both of them shall die.

³⁵ But I will raise up for Myself a [c]faithful priest who will do according to what is in My heart and in My soul; and I will build him a permanent and enduring house, and he will walk before My anointed [d]forever. 36 And it will happen that everyone who is left in your house will come and bow down to him for a piece of silver and a loaf of bread and say, "Please assign me to one of the priest's offices so I may eat a piece of bread."

SUMMARY OF THE REPERCUSSION:

1. God will cut off Eli's strength and the strength of his father's house.

2. There will never be any man living a long life in Eli's family. Men will die at young ages.

3. Men will die at the prime of life — there is dying prematurely, and there is dying at the prime of life!

4. Eli's two sons, Hophni and Phinehas, who caused these grievous sins against God, would die the same day.

5. Another priest would be raised from another family, which is entirely different from Eli's family.

6. Those left in Eli's family after the tragic deaths of Eli and his sons would beg for positions and food from the new priest. This is a curse, a reversal of

office and roles. Eli's grandchildren would also pay for this grievous sin against God; they would beg for bread from someone they should have been feeding. What an evil reversal of roles, a falling from grace to grass! This is similar to the Words in Ecclesiastes 10:7 (AMP): *"7 I have seen slaves riding on horses and princes walking like slaves on the ground."*

CHAPTER EIGHT

Take Action

The book of Genesis 40 explains the story of a man who was identified as the king's baker, and I would like to mention that this man also engaged in the sleep of death. I admonish you to read the entire chapter to enjoy and learn other lessons from all the characters mentioned.

The king of Egypt, at that time, was extremely angry with both his chief butler and the chief baker. He was so angry that he confined these two big officials to prison. These two men were sent to prison; at the same time, Joseph was already serving time for an offense he did not commit. Joseph was in charge of serving these two officials of the king. Then, there was a day Joseph went to serve these two men, and they both looked sad and depressed. Joseph, being a good man of God, was not carefree and insensitive to these men's countenances; neither did he shrug his shoulders, look away, and just carry out his daily duties or routines. It would, in a way, have been "the sleep of death" because eventually, minding the business of these men or caring for and meeting their needs led to his promotion and the actualization of God's plans for his life.

A good lesson from Joseph's reaction is that no matter the problem anyone is going through, do not close your bowels of mercy or be so buried in your problems. Learn to carry your cross, and while you are praying and still going through the challenges, take steps to solve your problems and learn to help others going through life's challenges. Helping others despite bearing the burdens of their challenges may open doors of solutions for you. Joseph eventually got his breakthrough by solving the problems of these two men.

What problem did they have? These two men had dreams on the same night. Being big officials of Pharaoh, they probably spoke to each other and learned about each other's dreams. They were both depressed and sad, as earlier mentioned, especially because there was no interpreter to interpret their dreams. They did not know Joseph could interpret dreams, and Joseph encouraged them to share their dreams, knowing that the Lord would interpret their dreams through him. The baker's part of the dream is in the book of Genesis

40:6-8, 16-19.

"⁶ When Joseph came to them in the morning and looked at them, [he saw that] they were sad and depressed. ⁷ So he asked Pharaoh's officials who were in confinement with him in his master's house, "Why do you look so down-hearted today?" ⁸ And they said to him, "We have [each] dreamed [distinct] dreams, and there is no one to interpret them." So Joseph said to them, "Do not interpretations belong to God? Please tell me [your dreams]."

"¹⁶ When the chief baker saw that the interpretation [of the dream] was good, he said to Joseph, "I also dreamed, and [in my dream] there were three cake baskets on my head; ¹⁷ and in the top basket there were some of all sorts of baked food for Pharaoh, but the birds [of prey] were eating [these foods] out of the basket on my head." ¹⁸ Joseph answered, "This is the interpretation of it: the three baskets represent three days; ¹⁹ within three more days Pharaoh will [a] lift up your head and will hang you on a tree (gallows, pole), and [you will not so much as be given a burial, but] the birds will eat your flesh."

When the chief baker saw that the interpretation Joseph gave to the chief butler was good, he summoned the courage to narrate his dream, as seen in verse 16 above. Then, the Holy Spirit showed me that the chief baker slept the sleep of death. I would implore you to pay careful attention to how this chief baker slept the sleep of death.

According to the Bible passage, it shows that this man was not an ordinary man or baker. He carried not one but three baskets of baked food. A great entrepreneur! The man carried what I likened to assorted anointing, entrepreneurial grace, multi-dimensional grace, and capability for multiple sources of income! The top basket on the baker's head had assorted pastries from the bakery, specially made for the king. A Biblical interpretation interpreted the assorted pastries as foods made by the art of baking — a special work of art of a baker. This showed a well-prepared man who was solid and sound in his career. He was not a novice or mediocre. He was astute and knowledgeable in his field; no wonder he was the king's chief baker.

How, then, did such a knowledgeable man engage in the sleep of death?

Let's examine the following together:

- The man saw birds of prey fly upon his head, not

across his head. The birds landed on the basket on his head!

- The birds began to eat from the basket carried by this man. It was Martin Luther who said, "You cannot keep birds from flying over your head, but you can keep them from building a nest in your hair." In this man's case, the birds did more than build a nest; they were feasting on his head.

- The birds were eating not just anybody's food; they were eating the food meant for "King Pharaoh." To Egyptians, Pharaoh was like a god. They treated him like a god.

- This Chief Baker did not drive the birds; rather, he allowed them to eat and there was no sharp reaction from him to drive the birds away!

- Joseph interpreted the dream in verse 19 as this, *"Within three more days Pharaoh will [a] lift up your head and will hang you on a tree (gallows, pole), and [you will not so much as be given a burial, but] the birds will eat your flesh."*

- When the baker was told that the king would hang him on a pole and kill him, and there would not even be any burial, and also, the birds would not be eating his baked goods but would eat him up! What did the baker do to avert this interpretation from coming to pass? NOTHING! The baker probably resigned himself to fate, and he was expecting death, as interpreted by Joseph!

- This is almost similar to Eli's reaction in 1 Samuel 3:18, *"Then Eli said, "He is the LORD; let him do what is good in his eyes."*

To me, the action of the baker in his case could be termed the sleep of death. What was the consequence of the baker's sleep of death? It's recorded in the same chapter, verse 22, *"but Pharaoh hanged the chief baker,"* just as Joseph had interpreted. The butler was restored to his original position, while the baker was hanged.

I pray that you will not experience the sleep of death. You will not be a "do nothing" where you should rise to action. You will not be passive when you should be active. You will not be reactive when you should be proactive. The excellence of the chief baker took him to the king's palace, but he ended up in jail and on the gallows. This is one of the tragedies of sleeping the sleep of death. You will not fall from your place of prominence. You will advance in Jesus' name. The baker slept the sleep of death, and his career and life ended abruptly. The sleep of death can be very devastating and must be rejected daily through prayers.

CHAPTER NINE

Examples of Some Spiritually Alert Women

There are some women in the Bible that I particularly love how they looked out for their children by being daring and alert. They took bold steps and made some demands to position their children in prominent places. I believe these women refused to be careless or allow things to slide, and truth be told, their actions inspired me. The actions taken by these women might not be pleasing to some individuals; however, I like what every one of them did, and I will back my explanation with the Scriptures.

Before discussing these women, let me share my personal life experience with you. I believe every woman has a womb to give birth to the destinies of their children, husband, and career, rewrite family histories, and set new standards for family lineages. I believe this can be achieved on their knees as they pray daily.

The future of your husband, children, and great-grandchildren (yet to be born), as well as the entire lineage, can be determined on your knees to give birth to the future now! Every day, I pray singularly for all my children. By the grace of God, I have ten children and raised them all. I mention their names one by one and pray according to what I know about them, and I also allow the Holy Spirit to guide me. I do not think parents should lump the names of their children together in prayer because children have different personalities, challenges, and destinies.

As a mother, I take time to pray for their future spouses and spend extra time praying for those who are already married, as led by the Holy Spirit. Honestly, I want to say in humility that the Lord is helping me to be alert and to give birth to the future of my family now; I cannot afford to sleep the sleep of death. I, however, still pray daily that God should help me not to experience the sleep of death in any area of my life. I have had many experiences of being attacked by the enemy in some of the encounters I had in my dreams, and it is evident that it was because I did not sleep the sleep of death. There were very few occurrences where the enemy was able to carry out certain evil steps, but God, in His mercy, gave me victories at the end.

If you are a young lady (whether married, with children, or expecting your children) reading this, I admonish you to refuse to let things lie low. Do not engage in the sleep of death by waiting for things to happen. Be proactive and give birth to the future of your loved ones now. It is never too late, and it is better to start now than to postpone. You may not like what is currently going on in some areas of your life. Perhaps you may be thinking, I already slept too many sleeps of death, and things are upside down. I can assure you that our God can turn things around, and He will turn things "right side up" and change all negative stories to work out for your good and the good of your family. Now that you know better, join the group of God's children who are refusing to experience the sleep of death and set a new family standard now.

Let's look at a few women from the Bible who did not engage in the sleep of death, based on my opinion. The first woman I want to discuss is **SALOME**, the mother of the Zebedee brothers. I am intrigued by the boldness and the action of this lady. You will find the story in Matthew 20:20-23 (AMP).

> *"20 Then [Salome] the [a]mother of Zebedee's children [James and John] came up to Jesus with her sons and, kneeling down [in respect], asked a favor of Him. 21 And He said to her, "What do you wish?" She answered Him, "Command that in Your kingdom these two sons of mine may sit [in positions of honor and authority] one on Your right and one on Your left."*
>
> *22 But Jesus replied, "You do not realize what you are asking. Are you able to drink the cup [of suffering] that I am about to drink?" They answered, "We are able." 23 He said to them, "You will drink My cup [of suffering]; but to sit on My right and on My left this is not Mine to give, but it is for those for whom it has been prepared by My Father."*

Here in this story, I love the way Mrs. Zebedee took her two boys to the Lord. You must do this with anyone or anything you care about — do not say God understands your need; take everything and everyone to the Lord in prayer daily. Do you notice what our Lord asked Salome? Jesus said, *"What do you wish?"* Wow, this is the open cheque God has given to every single believer — your wish. Matthew 7:7 says (KJV), *"Ask, and it shall be given you; seek and ye shall find; knock and it shall be opened unto you."*

Ask for whatever you want, open your heart to God in prayer, and let Him help you sort out the prayers. If you are asking for a wish "amiss," God knows how not to answer the prayer. Like Jesus did in the case of Salome. It would have been better to ask for the evil arrows of my enemies to backfire on them than for me to sleep the sleep of death and have my enemies prevail against me.

Let's look at how Mrs. Zebedee did not sleep the sleep of death:

1. Mrs. Zebedee asked our Lord to "Command that in His kingdom." It showed she was a woman of faith — she believed Jesus had the power to command her demands.

2. Salome Zebedee took the "bull by the horn" and stepped forward to ask Jesus to create positions of honor and authority for her two sons. She wanted her two sons to sit on Jesus' left and right sides! I love it! She was bold in her request. The Bible says in Hebrews 4:16 that we should be bold to approach God's throne. As I wrote earlier, it is better to ask and allow God to sort out the answers than not to ask at all. God told David that if he wanted more, he could have asked, and God would have sorted the

answers. My father has given me the open cheque, and it is better to maximize it for me and my loved ones by asking for everything. God knows how to sort out the answers to my prayers.

3. Mrs. Zebedee was a woman of faith, and going to Jesus directly revealed faith in action. There were instances in the Bible when people went to the disciples so that the disciples could talk to Jesus on their behalf. Not so with Mrs. Zebedee; she went straight to the Lord! According to Proverbs 28:1 (KJV), the Bible says, "The righteous are as bold as a lion." Whatever you need in life, go for it boldly, and if the front desk personnel are not delivering your request, do not just turn back and leave; ask for the leader of the organization.

4. The Zebedee brothers were not insignificant among the disciples; they were very active. However, their mother was shooting for a better future for them. The woman knew there would be a future kingdom, and she wanted to fix the future for her children. It's like she was saying, "I know there is a future kingdom, and I do not want these boys of mine to be ordinary men in that kingdom." I am looking out for their future now! Salome was taking care to arrange a promising future for her children. This is worthy of emulation; plan and take action for the bright future of your children, grandchildren, and

great-grandchildren yet to come.

Do not engage in the sleep of death. Do not wait till your children are grown before you pray certain prayers or take certain godly actions. Start praying about their careers, spouses, and life from the beginning of their lives. Some people wait until their children are grown adults before they start praying for them or taking action steps that should have been taken years before. You must take the bull by the horns, like Salome Zebedee.

5. Mrs. Zebedee did not worry about the reactions of the other ten disciples. Notice that the other ten disciples were angry about the step taken by their colleagues' mother. According to verse 21, without being insensitive to people around you, prayerfully go for your godly heart's desires. You cannot always get people to celebrate you as you forge forward in life, and everyone will not always agree with you.

There are times you must not care in your sleep, whom you "slam dunk" or shatter into pieces. There was a dream I had one time when the enemy came to attack me in my sleep, but the person appeared as one of my loved ones, someone I would never say "No" to, no matter the request my loved one put forth. Thank God for the Holy Spirit, who already fortified my spirit; this enemy who appeared as my loved one offered me one of my delicious meals, but the Holy Spirit quickly showed me that it was a "veiled" face to cover the natural person. It was not my loved one at all, and what I was being offered was not a good one. Needless to say, I did not eat the food. You must constantly ask God to make your spirit turn into a ball of fire and be dangerous, destructive, and aggressive against anyone coming to injure you or your loved ones. I pray you will not get carried away and sleep the sleep of death.

6. Lastly, notice that Jesus did not rebuke Mrs. Zebedee for making this request, and He did not deny her. Jesus said it was not in His power to make this decision. Wow, what a mother! I was not surprised to see that Jesus took the two boys with Him to the garden of Gethsemane —their mother did not engage in the sleep of death. She must have been praying and standing in the gap for her children. Please, as much as you can, pray over everything and take appropriate actions to secure a great future spiritually, financially, and eternally for your children.

Another example of a woman who did not sleep the sleep of death was **BATHSHEBA**, in the book of 1 Kings Chapter 1. Adonijah, one of King David's sons, projected himself as the next king after David. David was old at this time, but he had not officially declared the person who would be crowned king among his children. Nathan, the priest, arranged with Bathsheba how she should get her son (Solomon) to be the king. Bathsheba had to go to King David to remind him of his promise concerning Solomon. In 1 Kings 1:17-18 (NIV), Bathsheba went to David and said, *"My lord, you yourself swore to me your servant by the LORD your God: 'Solomon your son shall be king after me, and he will sit on my throne.' ^{18} But now Adonijah has become king, and you, my lord the king, do not know about it."*

In response to the action Bathsheba took to speak up for her son, Solomon, **that same day**, Solomon was made the king over Israel and Judah according to 1 Kings 1:30. Solomon became the king, and all the funfair and parties thrown by Adonijah were nullified. In fact, on the same day, he went to bow before Solomon (1 Kings 1:53).

POINTS TO CONSIDER

- Bathsheba did not waste time yielding to the advice of Nathan, the priest.

- Bathsheba went to King David and reminded him of his promise concerning Solomon.

- Parents (in this case, mothers) should listen to the Word of God from the priest.

JOCHEBED, Moses' mother, was also another example of a spiritually alert woman. When Pharaoh **ordered death warrants over babies and little boys of the Jewish nation. She decided to hide her baby from the executioners and devised a means to rescue him. She even watched over him so he could land into a safe hand** (Exodus 2:1-3, NIV).

> *"¹ Now a man of the tribe of Levi married a Levite woman, ² and she became pregnant and gave birth to a son. When she saw that he was a fine child, she hid him for three months. ³ But when she could hide him no longer, she got a papyrus basket[a] for him and coated it with tar and pitch. Then she placed the child in it and put it among the reeds along the bank of the Nile."*

What a dynamic, innovative, and caring mother this woman was! She did not sleep the sleep of death. Jochebed was very alert and sensitive in Spirit and she took very drastic actions to save the life of her son. Pay attention to some of the actions this woman took to prevent the termination of her son's destiny.

Like Jochebed, who did not sleep the sleep of death but was spiritually sensitive, today's parents must also not sleep the sleep of death. Jochebed hid Moses, so parents should do everything in their power to hide and protect their children from the "god" of this age (Satan is the god of this age) or systems that might want to lure children, indoctrinate them, and kill them.

Below are some of the qualities Jochebed exhibited that reflected her spiritual sensitivity.

1. **Jochebed was a perceiver (Exodus 2:2) because she saw something special in her child, Moses.**

   - This quality of perception will help you stay alert and properly decode people and events around you.

   - Perception is the spirit of discerning (1 Corinthians 12:10). The Jewish people were spiritually slothful. They slept the sleep of death and missed their Messiah (Jesus) because they looked at Jesus superficially, and they erroneously decoded His person.

   - Perception is the ability to see beyond the outward appearance or the physical (2 Kings 4:9). Both male and female singles should emulate this virtue.

   - Some singles capitalize on having a chemistry connection, in this case. Though it is not a bad thing to have chemistry connectivity, singles should pray to be perceivers.

SPIRITUAL SLUMBER

- Some singles have been slothful and spiritually careless and have unknowingly slept the sleep of death due to their lack of perception.

2. **Jochebed was a wise and strategic woman.**

    - Being wise will help you strategically to resist slothfulness. Someone defined wisdom as the application of sound knowledge. It is knowing what to do and doing it well. Jochebed, in her wisdom, knew she could not hide a newborn baby for too long, so she took necessary action, according to Exodus 2:3.

    - Jochebed knew there were different seasons and times of life and understood that this phase of her child's life needed to be hidden.

    - Young mothers, this is a call for you to be wise and strategic. Your children will not be with you forever, just like Moses was with Jochebed for only three months. Time flies fast; children are with their parents for a short time. As Jochebed did not sleep the sleep of death by making baskets for Moses, make baskets for your children. Jochebed did not just toss Moses into a basket; she prepared the basket with special waterproof materials.

It is just a fact of life that your children will soon be

thrown into the Nile. Inside the Nile of life are the alligators, snakes, whales, sharks, and many uncertainties as a result of social media, ungodly friends, and evolution and science hypotheses.

It is not only the children who should be basketed. To avoid sleeping the sleep of death or spiritual slumber, build baskets or barricades around everything and everyone connected to you. Many marriages have been ruined because one or both spouses experienced the sleep of death. Many children's destinies are vandalized and truncated due to parental and caregivers' slothfulness and spiritual slumber. So, we need to be spiritually discerning at all times. May God help us. Amen!

CHAPTER TEN

Examples of People Who Slept the Sleep of Death

As much as there are examples of those who are spiritually sensitive to the circumstances around them, there are still examples of people who experienced the sleep of death. I would like to explain a few points from their experiences so they could serve as lessons for us and make us watchful Christians.

1. **Peter, James, and John (Matthew 26:38, AMP)**

   "38 Then He said to them, "My soul is deeply grieved, so that I am almost dying of sorrow. Stay here and stay awake and keep watch with Me."

SPIRITUAL SLUMBER

While Jesus asked some of His disciples to stay behind, He took these three disciples, Peter, James, and John, with Him to pray. Jesus asked these three disciples to pray at a very crucial time of His life. Instead of these trusted disciples to pray, they slept! They physically slept when they should be praying. Three times, Jesus asked them to pray.

In my subjective opinion, I think you will know that these disciples were not spiritually alert. They were asleep spiritually before sleep overtook them physically. In Matthew 26:38, they were spiritually slothful and slept the sleep of death when they missed both the tone and the Words of Jesus. Jesus said His soul was deeply grieved and that he was almost dying of sorrow! The disciples should have caught a deeper interpretation of this verse that Jesus never sounded like that before, and it must be important for them to pray.

The second time, Jesus said in verses 40-41 (AMP), *"40 And He came to the disciples and found them sleeping, and said to Peter, "So, you men could not stay awake and keep watch with Me for one hour? 41 Keep actively watching and praying that you may not come into temptation; the spirit is willing, but the [a] body is weak."* These words should have also alerted them that temptation was along the way and that they should obey Jesus. The three disciples, however, engaged in the sleep of death, slothfulness, carelessness, and insensitivity.

The spiritual slumber continued throughout the stay of Jesus and the disciples on the mountain, according to Matthew 26:43-46. Jesus' heart was heavy, but the eyes of the disciples were heavy, and not their heart. They slept spiritually and physically. This sleep of death caused them heavily later when Jesus was arrested. The Bible says in Matthew 26:56b (AMP), *"Then all the disciples deserted Him and fled."* Being spiritually insensitive can be very costly, and in this case, people who should be bold and stand with Jesus fled out of fear.

Ponder on this: When you have experienced spiritual slumber in secret, you will run and be in fear in the daylight. A slothful believer, sleeping the sleep of death, will run when nobody is chasing. The people came for Jesus, not for His disciples!

Sleeping the sleep of death, which is equal to spiritual slothfulness or spiritual insensitivity, is very deadly and costly.

- It can make a fervent believer who used to cling to Jesus to follow Jesus from afar. Check Peter's action in Matthew 26:58.
- The "follow Jesus from afar" believer will not only deny Jesus but will swear to confirm the

seriousness of his denial (Matthew 26:72).

- There are many ways sleeping the sleep of death can cause 21st-century believers to deny Jesus and even swear for attestation. Therefore, it is important for us as believers to always be watchful.

Permit me to buttress this explanation with the real-life story of Mr. and Mrs. Sloppy (name undisclosed). An unfortunate experience occurred a few years ago in the lives of Mr. and Mrs. Sloppy, living in the diaspora. Mr. Sloppy had a beautiful property built on his behalf by his older brother, and the property was attractive to behold. Unfortunately, a rift occurred between the two brothers as it became evident that Mr. Sloppy's older brother did not want to release the documents of ownership to Mr. Sloppy. While the brothers were still at loggerheads on the matter, Mr. Sloppy died mysteriously and suddenly. Mrs. Sloppy was very devastated, especially because there were rumors that the older brother had caused the untimely death of her husband. After a while, Mrs. Sloppy discussed her decision to travel to her birth country for the document with her brother-in-law. She traveled eventually, and the documents were released to her by her brother-in-law. She was quite surprised at the ease with which she collected what her husband could not collect. She planned to travel the next day, but another unusual thing happened.

Mrs. Sloppy never woke up; she died in her sleep! By the way, Mrs. Sloppy was a very healthy, young, and vibrant lady. It was, however, discovered that Mr. Sloppy came from a family of voodoo-believing and practicing religion. Mrs. Sloppy slept the sleep of death that led to her actual physical death. Recall, the sleep of death is the kind of sleep people engage in and terrible things are done to them or things belonging to them. In this case, they are passive or inactive until the enemy has carried out his evil works. It is sweeping and sleeping away mentally, spiritually, and sometimes even physically.

2. The Five Foolish Virgins

Although they were virgins, they were spiritually slothful.

> *"1 Then the kingdom of heaven will be like ten virgins, who took their lamps and went to [a]meet the bridegroom. 2 Five of them were foolish [thoughtless, silly, and careless], and five were wise [far-sighted, practical, and sensible]. 3 For when the foolish took their lamps, they did not take any [extra] oil with them."* (Matthew 25:1-3, AMP)

These five foolish virgins were portraying obedience to

Christ by waiting for the bridegroom, but not having extra oil in their lamps shows that they were thoughtless and careless about the activities around them. It is possible to be doing some good things while you are spiritually asleep to other important things in life. Be alert and prepared!

3. Eglon, King of Moab, and His Servants (Judges 3:19-23)

There was a king who was so careless and spiritually insensitive to the mission of the guests who went into his palace. The king's name was Eglon, the king of Moab. God raised Ehud to deliver His people. Ehud pretended he had a gift for the king, and he gave the king the gift but claimed he had another message from God to Eglon. Eglon slept the sleep of death due to his carelessness and was also spiritually insensitive, so he instructed all his servants to leave the room. This left Ehud to be alone with the king, and Ehud was able to kill Eglon.

Similarly, Eglon's servants were also insensitive because they did not attend to their work with due diligence and seriousness. Their master was not only successfully killed, but also their spiritual slothfulness and sleep of death allowed Ehud to escape (Judges 3:23). It was a good thing King Eglon of Moab was killed because he was an enemy of God's people. This point is just to explain the subject matter. They waited too long to check on their master. Spiritual insensitivity will make you linger where you should not; it will make you speak in situations where you should have been quiet and just make you do things outside of your regular time.

4. Commander Sisera (Judges 4)

This commander of the Canaanite army had about 900 iron chariots, including other foot soldiers. God defeated the enemies of His children and caused confusion among Sisera's army (verse 15).

Sisera, however, slept the sleep of death. He slept physically and plunged to his death at the hands of a woman, Jael, according to Judges 4:17 (AMP).

> *"17 But Sisera fled on foot to the tent of Jael, the wife of Heber the Kenite, because there was peace between Jabin the king of Hazor and the house of Heber the Kenite. 18 Jael went out to meet Sisera, and said to him, "Turn aside, my lord, turn aside to me! Have no fear." So he turned aside to her [and went] into the tent, and she covered him with a rug. 19 And he said to her, "Please give me a little water to drink because I am thirsty." And she opened a skin of milk and gave him a drink; then she covered him.*

> *[20] And he said to her, "Stand at the door of the tent, and if any man comes and asks you, 'Is there anyone here?' tell him, 'No.'" [21] But Jael, Heber's wife, took a tent peg and a hammer in her hand, and came up quietly to him and drove the peg through his temple, and it went through into the ground; for he was sound asleep and exhausted. So he died."*

From the story, Sisera laid down and drank milk while he was still at war! Who does that? There is a time for everything under the sun. However, it must have been the hand of God that caused a whole commander of a mighty army to turn into a tent to drink milk, lay down, and then sleep! Spiritual slothfulness will make you lay down when you should be up and alert. It could even make you eat and drink when you ought to be fasting. Though this story was a story of victory for the Israelites, I am only opening our eyes to how people can engage in spiritual slumber.

5. Saul, the First King of Israel

> *"[6] Then David said to Ahimelech the Hittite and to Abishai the son of Zeruiah, brother of Joab, "Who will go down with me to Saul in the camp?" And Abishai said, "I will go down with you." [7] So David and Abishai went to the army during the night, and there*

> *was Saul lying asleep inside the circle of the camp with his spear stuck in the ground by his head; and Abner and the people were lying around him."* (1 Samuel 26:6-7, AMP)

The Bible recorded that Saul was fast asleep, as well as all the men around him, including the commander of his army! Everybody was in a deep sleep. Without even reading verse 12, knowing how God defends His children, it should be obvious that it was the hand of the Lord that would make about 3000 warriors fall asleep knowing their enemy was close by! The lessons in the Scripture point out the fact that **our God is a mighty man in battle, and He knows how to put your enemies to sleep. Sometimes, God will even make the enemies fight themselves or make them flee when nobody is running after them!**

In this passage, David could have killed Saul, and all his wandering would have been over. In fact, Abishai was a fearless warrior who would have pinned Saul with the spear only once, as he said in verse 8. However, David, a man who feared the Lord, would not touch the Lord's anointed (verse 11-12, AMP).

> *"11 The LORD forbid that I would put out my hand against the LORD's anointed; but now take the spear that is by his head and the jug*

> *of water, and let us go." ⁱ² So David took the spear and the jug of water from beside Saul's head, and they left, and no one saw or knew nor did anyone awaken,* because they were all sound asleep, for a deep sleep from the Lord *had fallen on them."*

- David took Saul's spear and the jug of water as evidence that he could have killed Saul, but he just did not.

- Was the deep sleep from God to see what was in David's heart? Was it a test that David passed just like he did? The death of Saul would have given him a faster way to the throne, but it would have had many consequences. So, David reflected the character of Christ and waited for the timing of the Lord.

Saul and his people slept the sleep of death, and it could have cost all of them their lives! Spiritual slumber will make the most powerful become so vulnerable and powerless. The scenario also reflects a group of people, community, church, family, or anyone in slothfulness, carelessness, and in a deep sleep of death. This kind of sleep breaks the edge around a family, group, or church. When the edge is broken, it leaves all entries open for the devil to come in and make minced meat of the careless group. It is my prayer that you will not sleep the sleep of death. May your family and church not sleep a collective sleep of death in Jesus' name.

6. The Deep Sleep of Jonah

How can you fall into a deep sleep knowing you are running away from God and His assignment? This was what Jonah did. As Christians, you need to get up and call on God! The truth is you can never run away from God, so the best decision you could make is to surrender all to him and see how He sorts things out for you.

This is one strategy you can embark upon and employ to prevent the sleep of death. Jonah was in a deep sleep, and the boat he was sailing in was capsizing! (Jonah 1:5-6). Even unbelievers in the same boat as Jonah were calling on whatever or whoever they saw as god. Jonah, who had a covenant with the only Almighty God, went to a deep sleep. It was not even an ordinary sleep; it was a deep one.

SPIRITUAL SLUMBER

I am subjectively of the opinion that this deep sleep must have come from the evil one, and it could mean several things in the life of a believer.

- It may mean that a believer is backsliding from God and has been blinded by Satan. Imagine that the same God you have trusted, who saved you, helped you, provided for you, healed you, and protected you from your enemies, is now the God you are so far away from.

- You may be far away and in deep sleep due to comfort. The riches and change of status, children, marriage, and business God has given you are now taking too much of your time, and you are insensitive to pray and study God's Words.

CHAPTER ELEVEN

Practical Ways to Prevent the Sleep of Death

As a believer, you should bear in mind that God wants His children to enjoy their physical sleep and avoid spiritual slumber. So, you need to know God's will for your life when it comes to physical sleep and spiritual apathy or the sleep of death. The will of God for His children is to have good rest and sweet sleep when it comes to physical sleep and to be very alert and conscious to avoid the sleep of death. There are many Scriptures a believer can read, memorize, or stand upon to enjoy physical sleep. Scriptures such as: Psalm 127:2, Psalm 4:8, Ecclesiastes 5:12, Proverbs 3:5, Jeremiah 31:26.

With the assurance in these Bible passages, you should understand that God wants His children to enjoy sweet and pleasant rest. He does not want us to turn and toss around because He, Himself, grants the believers' sleep. If your sleep time is a struggle, call upon the Lord, meditate on God's promises, and also engage in activities that can calm you at night. Sometimes, when people are troubled, anxious, or in despair, they may find it difficult to sleep. When Nebuchadnezzar had some trouble sleeping, the Bible says in Daniel 2:1 (ESV), *"his sleep left him."* There are times, even as believers, that one can be troubled, anxious, or be in what I call the valleys of life experiences. In such times, believers can study, memorize, and meditate upon the Words of God to enjoy the sweet rest God designed for His children. Scriptures such as Psalm 127:2, and Psalm 3:3-6 can be memorized.

Based on the subject matter of this book, God wants us to be spiritually alert, and there are many ways believers can avoid being slothful in the Spirit. These include some of the things to know and do to avoid the sleep of death.

ESSENTIAL FACTORS REQUIRED TO AVOID THE SLEEP OF DEATH

1. Know the Will of God

You must know that it is God's will for you to avoid sleeping the sleep of death. Jesus died for believers to be victorious in all areas over the devil. The devil is a fallen being, and he has fallen under the believer's feet. Jesus said in Luke 10:18 (AMP), *"¹⁸ He said to them, "I watched Satan fall from heaven like [a flash of] lightning."*

My subjective opinion of this verse is that if the devil fell like lightning, it was a very bad fall that put the devil under the believer's feet. Come to think of it; science taught us that light travels at the speed of 186,000 miles per second, so this implies that Satan fell at the speed of light! He is a **defeated, deflated, and depowered being!** A newborn baby believer who knows the will of God and applies the power of Christ will not fall for any deception that may lead to sleeping the sleep of death.

Many Scriptures show God's will for His children and that God does not want believers to be defeated or fall into spiritual slumber. Knowing the will of God regarding spiritual slothfulness can be appropriated daily by meditating, memorizing, praying, or reciting some of these Scriptures.

Such Scriptures include:

a. **1 Peter 5:8 (NIV)** - *"⁸ Be alert and of sober mind. Your enemy the devil prowls around like a roaring lion looking for someone to devour."*

b. **1 Thessalonians 5:6 (AMP)** - *"⁶ So then let us not sleep [in spiritual indifference] as the rest [of the world does], but let us keep wide awake [alert and cautious] and let us be sober [self-controlled, calm, and wise]."*

- As you pray, remind yourself that it is God's will for you not to sleep the sleep of death.

- If something is God's will, then we as believers should not settle for the less of God's will for our lives.

c. **1 Corinthians 10:13 (NIV)** - *"¹³ No temptation has overtaken you except what is common to mankind. And God is faithful; he will not let you be tempted beyond what you can bear. But when you are tempted, he will also provide a way out so that you can endure it."*

d. **1 Corinthians 15:57 (AMP)** - *"⁵⁷ But thanks be to God, who gives us the victory [as conquerors] through our Lord Jesus Christ."*

e. **2 Corinthians 2:14 (AMP)** - *"¹⁴ But thanks be to God, who always leads us in triumph in Christ, and through us spreads and makes evident everywhere the* *sweet fragrance of the knowledge of Him."*

The believer who wants to use this weaponry can recite any of the above Scriptures:

> *Father, I thank you as I step out today and run around. I decree I will be spiritually alert. In the name of Jesus, I will not sleep the sleep of death. I affirm the Word of God in 1 Thessalonians 5:6 upon my life. I am calm, wise, and alert. I will not sleep like the rest of the world. The enemy may go around like a roaring lion, but I am the child of the Lion of Judah, Jesus Christ. I overcome the devil's plots and plans today in Jesus' name.*

2. Possess the Gates of the Enemy by Resisting the Devil

To avoid engaging in the sleep of death, you need to possess the gates of the enemy. Knowing the strategies and ways of your enemy, the opponent, and developing action plans to counter these strategies is a sure winning ticket. As everyone wakes up daily to do their job, pursue their dreams in life, and carry out activities for the day, Satan, being a spirit, also has a job. The devil also goes around doing his evil job. The Lord Jesus told us in John 10:10 (AMP), *"¹⁰ The thief comes only in order to steal and kill and destroy. I came that they may have and enjoy life, and have it in abundance [to the full, till it overflows]."*

Believers in the Lord Jesus can possess the gates of the enemy through all the points written in this chapter. Possess the gates of the enemy by using all the spiritual weapons given to the believer in the Bible. Some verses to strengthen the believer's faith include, but are not limited to the following:

a. **1 Peter 5:8-9 (NIV)** - *"⁸ Be alert and of sober mind. Your enemy the devil prowls around like a roaring lion looking for someone to devour. ⁹ Resist him, standing firm in the faith, because you know that the family of believers throughout the world is undergoing the same kind of sufferings."*

In the verse above, you can possess the gates of the enemy by resisting the devil. There are many ways to resist the devil, which can be found in the Scripture above.

- Firstly, be humble under the mighty hand of the Lord (1 Peter 5:6). You are only able to resist the devil through the power of God. The power of God can be released in you and through you by being vulnerable and humble to God.

- Cast your cares before the Lord.

- Be vigilant, and then, you can resist the devil.

b. **James 4:7 (NIV)** - *"⁷Submit yourselves, then, to God. Resist the devil, and he will flee from you."*

The believer, in this sense, must first submit to God. It is after submitting to God that you can be empowered and emboldened to resist the devil.

c. **Genesis 22:17 (AMP)** - *"¹⁷Indeed I will greatly bless you, and I will greatly multiply your descendants like the stars of the heavens and like the sand on the seashore; and your seed shall possess the gate of their enemies [as conquerors]."*

Other Bible verses include 1 John 4:4 and Isaiah 14:12. The believer can declare spiritual warfare against the devil by standing upon the promises of God in these verses. Ensure you pray these verses.

3. Practice the Presence of God

As a believer, you are a child of God, and this should assure you that you are not alone. As you go from place to place, know that Jesus is with you, so walk in this awareness more than the deception of Satan. Slap it in the face of the devil that you are not alone and that the devil cannot get you as he tries to lure you into sleeping the sleep of death.

Scriptures that show Jesus is with us always include:

- Hebrews 13:5
- Romans 8:38-39
- Zephaniah 3:17
- Matthew 28:20
- Isaiah 41:10

Using this weapon against sleeping the sleep of death can also be appropriated by being more aware of God's presence instead of being more aware of the presence of the evil one to tempt you.

Appropriate the power and the presence of God more than the strategies of the enemy to defeat you.

4. Walk Daily in the Authority of the Believer

Believers have been empowered and authorized to act as Jesus' representatives on earth. Jesus has delegated the power of attorney to believers to occupy and do the business of the kingdom till He comes back again. When a believer is aware of such empowerment and authority and knows his identity in Christ, it will be easy to exercise such authority and power against the schemes of the devil to distract the believer or cause the believer to be slothful.

Walking in the authority of the believer also means

having an understanding of what to do. Knowing what to do and doing it gives you power over the enemy. The psalmist in Psalm 13:3 (AMP) says, *"Consider and answer me, O LORD my God; Give light (life) to my eyes, or I will sleep the sleep of death."* "The light to the eyes" also means "give light to my situation and give me knowledge and understanding of what to do to solve the problems around me and in my life."

Some of the Scriptures that talk about the power and authority given to believers are:

- Luke 10:19
- Acts 1:8
- Luke 9:1
- Luke 10:17

To walk daily in the authority that has been given to us, you can write the Scriptures that resonate most with you. Staple the written Scriptures to walls or places where you can see and read them daily. Remind yourself that you have the power over the one who wants to lure you into spiritual slumber. Speak the Scriptures out with authority, and the devil will flee from you.

5. Know That the Holy Spirit of God Lives in You

Having the Spirit of God in a believer makes the

believer the most powerful person on earth! Jesus said in John 14:16-17 (AMP), *"¹⁶ And I will ask the Father, and He will give you another [a]Helper (Comforter, Advocate, Intercessor—Counselor, Strengthener, Standby), to be with you forever— ¹⁷ the Spirit of Truth, whom the world cannot receive [and take to its heart] because it does not see Him or know Him, but you know Him because He (the Holy Spirit) remains with you continually and will be in you."*

To avoid engaging in the sleep of death, try to understand the caliber of the Spirit of God who lives in you. The Bible says the Holy Spirit is your: Helper, Comforter, Advocate, Intercessor, Counselor, Strengthener, Standby, Guide, Teacher, Spirit of Truth, Spirit of Grace, Spirit of God, and Spirit of Christ. So, who is the devil to lure me into sleeping the sleep of death when the Holy Spirit of God, who is all the above and more, lives in me to help me? Also, the Holy Spirit sometimes prompts believers that if they pay attention to these warnings, they will not fall victim to any careless sleep.

Ask the Holy Spirit daily and at every moment to help you. Practically, you can talk to the Holy Spirit and ask Him to counsel you, guide you, and teach you to avoid the sleep of death. You can declare this prayer: Holy Spirit, I thank you for living in me. Thank you for being my ……… (mention some of the listed names above), and thank you for empowering me against the devil today. In the name of Jesus, as my standby helper and bodyguard, I will not sleep the sleep of death. Amen!

6. Learn to Honor God's Word and His Promises, and Do Not Tempt the Lord Your God

The devil is a master deceiver, crafty and evil. The Bible says the devil must not be given a foothold. Do not dialogue with the devil if you do not know the Word. Eve fell through dialoguing with the devil. The devil twisted God's Word, and Eve fell. The world is still paying for that deception. The devil also tried Jesus with the same deception of twisting God's Word and promises, according to Matthew 4:1-11. Jesus was not playing with the devil, and He was firm and stern in His response.

Similarly, Christians must not play with the devil. Do the "**Rs**" against the devil: do not **romance** his thoughts, do not **receive** his evil suggestions; **refuse, reject, repel, and refute** his evil suggestions.

7. Know How God Speaks to You and Obey God's Instructions

Be cognizant of how God speaks to you. God is a good God who speaks daily to His children. Find out the ways God speaks to you. Believers can avoid sleeping the sleep of death when they know how God speaks, and they obey. Know How God speaks to you and obey God's voice (these two must walk hand in hand). Hear, listen, and obey the voice of God. It will help you from sleeping the sleep of death.

The parents of Jesus obeyed and complied with God's instructions. When King Herod wanted to kill Jesus, the death was averted (Yes, Jesus could not be killed before His time) because Joseph and Mary obeyed the instructions of God. It would have been a sleep of death if Joseph and Mary had ignored God's instructions with the notion that Jesus was the Messiah and could not be killed regardless of Herod's plans. Herod's evil plan must have been devastating to Jesus or probably messed up God's plans. This must have been the reason God told Joseph and Mary to leave. Imagine if they were not sensitive to the instructions God gave them through dreams. Joseph and Mary received the message (Matthew 2:13), and they obeyed. I pray for you that as Herod, who was trying to terminate Jesus, was terminated, those who are trying to destroy you will be destroyed in Jesus' name.

As a child of God, you need to be very sensitive and know some of the ways God talks to people. He speaks to us in diverse ways, which are:

- *God speaks through dreams and visions (Joel 2:28)*

Your dreams are powerful, so pay attention to them. God warned Joseph, the earthly father of Jesus, through dreams in Matthew 2:13.

- *Through the inner witness of the Holy Spirit (John 14:26)*

In the book of Acts 16:6-7, the disciples were warned not to speak the Word of God in certain towns. Acts 16:6-7 (AMP) - *"⁶ Now they passed through the territory of Phrygia and Galatia, after being forbidden by the Holy Spirit to speak the word in [the west coast province of] Asia [Minor]; ⁷ and after they came to Mysia, they tried to go into Bithynia, but the Spirit of Jesus did not permit them;"*

A specific instruction by Jesus was stated clearly in Matthew 28:19-20. If you compare the assignment given by Christ and the experience of the disciples here, one may wonder how the Holy Spirit can warn the disciples not to do the assignment the Lord gave them. This is called being sensitive or being vigilant in the Spirit. The inner witnessing to any information is when the Holy Spirit directs you and confirms what the Lord has been dropping in your mind or when the Holy Spirit is directing you based on God's plans for your life and based on what is safe for your life.

For example, look at the passage above in Acts 16. It would look like the Holy Spirit was telling the disciples not to carry out and obey the instruction of Jesus based on the great commission. However, the Holy Spirit wanted the disciples to preach and obey Jesus, but the Spirit knew that the lives of the disciples might be in danger in those cities. Therefore, the Spirit warned them not to go to these cities. Let us assume the disciples disregarded the instruction of the Holy Spirit, and something bad happened to them. It would not be that God did not protect them; it would be that they were not sensitive to the voice of the Holy Spirit in them. Disobedience to the Holy Spirit when He speaks to us may lead to unnecessary hardships or bad experiences for a believer. Such insensitivities to the voice of God can be termed "sleeping the sleep of death." As a child of God, be sensitive to the inner witness, the inner voice of the Holy Spirit in your daily walk.

Some other ways God speaks include the following:

- God speaks through His written Words.

"All Scripture is given by inspiration of God, and is profitable for doctrine, for reproof, for correction, for instruction in righteousness" (2 Timothy 3:16, KJV). The Word of God is one of the various means that God uses to speak to us. Meditating on the Scriptures can open

our eyes and hearts to the instruction he wants to give us, the promises he wants us to claim, the command he wants us to follow, the prayers He wants us to pray, and a lot more.

- *God speaks through Pastors, Prophets, and Godly people. (Romans 12:6-8)*

- *God speaks through circumstances. (Exodus 3:2)*

- *God speaks through angels. (Matthew 2:13-14, Luke 1:13-17)*

- *God speaks through prayer - when you pray, cultivate the habit of listening to God. (Acts 13:2)*

- *God speaks through the gifts of the Holy Spirit. (1 Corinthians 12:1- 11)*

- *God speaks through His creations. (Psalm 19:1-2, Numbers 22:23-30)*

As a believer, be familiar with the voice of God and especially the specific ways God speaks to you. As you hear and obey His voice, God will lead you away from the devil's troubled waters of temptations to fall into sleeping the sleep of death. God will guide you into the still waters of life through the different ways He speaks to you.

8. Walk by Faith

Faith is having unshakable, undoubtedly, and unwavering trust in the **person** of God, His **plans** (Words), and His **promises.** Faith is having absolute belief in God and His Words. In order not to sleep the sleep of death, faith is an indispensable, daily weapon every believer must have. Everything in the kingdom is connected to faith, so faith is very vital in the walk of every believer.

In my opinion, faith is like the flour that holds the ingredients in a cake together. All the points shared about how to overcome sleeping the sleep of death in this chapter must be done in faith. When you pray, you have to believe in God, believe in His Words, believe that He hears you, and believe that your prayers will be answered. For a believer not to sleep the sleep of death, you must make faith a lifestyle. Ask God daily to walk by faith and to have faith to avoid the sleep of death. By faith, reject, do not receive, nor romance the deceptive thoughts the devil will shoot into your mind, wanting you to be slothful.

Ephesians 6:16 (NIV) says, *"⁶ In addition to all this, take up the **shield of faith,** with which you can extinguish all the flaming arrows of the evil one."* The shield of faith is a part of the armory of God that believers are admonished to wear to fight the evil one. The shield of faith is a defensive weapon that fights off or deflects fiery darts, flaming arrows the enemy shoots to lure the believer into a deep sleep of death. Flaming arrows can come in the form of negative thoughts, temptations, deception, distraction, lies, and anything the enemy can use to steal, kill, or destroy. Faith can be taken up by refuting all the advances of Satan and standing on the promises of God.

Scriptures showing the importance of faith include:

- Believers are saved by grace through faith. (Ephesians 2:8)

- Believers are to walk by faith, not by sight. (2 Corinthians 5:7)

- Believers can only please God by faith. (Hebrews 11:2)

Other Scriptures on the importance of faith are Mark 11:24, James 5:14-15, James 1:6, Mark 9:23, and Matthew 17:20.

9. Habitually Wear the Whole Armor of God Daily

The Bible says in Ephesians 6:10-17 that believers are

to put on the whole armor of God. Be fully dressed, not scantily dressed. Do not wear one without the other to be victorious against the devices of the devil; you need to wear the full regalia daily. The whole armor of God is in Ephesians 6:10-17 (NIV).

> *"10 Finally, be strong in the Lord and in his mighty power. 11 Put on the full armor of God, so that you can take your stand against the devil's schemes. 12 For our struggle is not against flesh and blood, but against the rulers, against the authorities, against the powers of this dark world and against the spiritual forces of evil in the heavenly realms.*
>
> *13 Therefore put on the full armor of God, so that when the day of evil comes, you may be able to stand your ground, and after you have done everything, to stand. 14 Stand firm then, with the belt of truth buckled around your waist, with the breastplate of righteousness in place, 15 and with your feet fitted with the readiness that comes from the gospel of peace. 16 In addition to all this, take up the shield of faith, with which you can extinguish all the flaming arrows of the evil one. 17 Take the helmet of salvation and the sword of the Spirit, which is the word of God."*

10. Be Prayerful

Prayer is a very powerful spiritual tool with inexhaustible advantages. The God we serve is a prayer-hearing and prayer-answering God. Prayer takes you to the presence of God, and in the presence of God is EVERYTHING you need, including the grace to avoid sleeping the sleep of death. The believer must cultivate the habit of communicating with God daily because God will intervene and fortify the believer who prays daily about being spiritually alert. Prayer should not be seen as an uphill task, uninteresting, or a sanctimonious action. Jesus said in Matthew 7:7-8 (AMP), *"7 [a]Ask and keep on asking and it will be given to you; seek and keep on seeking and you will find; knock and keep on knocking and the door will be opened to you. 8 For everyone who keeps on asking receives, and he who keeps on seeking finds, and to him who keeps on knocking, it will be opened."*

Every seeker will eventually find what is being sought. The one who knocks the door will eventually get an open door. This is why it is important for you to present daily to God, during your prayer time, both the things you want or do not want in your life. Have faith that God hears and answers your prayers, and be aware of God's presence every day.

I believe that David was engaged in prayer when he penned Psalm 13:3-4 (AMP), *"3 Consider and answer me, O LORD my God; Give light (life) to my eyes, or I will sleep the sleep of death, ⁴And my enemy will say, "I have overcome him," And my adversaries will rejoice when I am shaken."*

We, too, must also take time to pray daily. Believers should be free to take EVERYTHING to God in prayers. Ask God for the grace to overcome temptations and strategies to overcome the devil. Take the opportunity to ask God for protection during the day. One must specifically ask the Lord for the grace of alertness in the Spirit and the grace to avoid sleeping the sleep of death.

One of the advantages of prayer can be seen in the book of John 14:13-14 (AMP), *"¹³ And I will do whatever you ask in My name [[a]as My representative], this I will do, so that the Father may be glorified and celebrated in the Son. ¹⁴ If you ask Me anything in My name [as My representative], I will do it."* The words "whatever and anything" are emboldened to show that, as Christians, we can ask **whatever and anything**. Nothing is too big or too small to ask the Lord in prayer. Jesus is saying, "Be assured that if you ask whatever or anything (in line with His Word) in His name, answers will be granted to us." In order not to experience the sleep of death, you can pray daily and ask God specifically to be alert during the day and guide you from insensitivity to the happenings around you.

God can answer your prayer in diverse ways. One way to receive such answers when you pray is to practice being silent in the presence of the Lord. As a believer, when you pray, have moments of being silent before God. In those quiet moments when you are not talking but listening, God gives you pictures, words, phrases, or verses that will be things to pay attention to during the day, month, or even the year. As a child of God, cultivate the habit of expecting God to talk to you during prayer. After all, prayer is communication between the believer and God. God does not want to hide anything from His children, but when the believer is in too much of a hurry during prayer, one may miss important moments of the Lord speaking to the believer. Some of these moments are when God warns us to be sensitive and vigilant about things that may happen to us and how to guard and arm ourselves for the day.

Let me buttress the point above with the story of a man of God called Andrew Wommack. He mentioned that he was invited to speak at a big church event. The flyer had already been printed, and return tickets were bought for him to travel to this big church program. The man of God said that after praying one morning, he began to feel restless about going to the same event he had originally thought he was led to attend. This man was convinced after his prayers that he should call his host, apologize, and cancel the trip. This man reluctantly and unhappily called his host, and he did not have any good reason at all for canceling the trip everybody had already prepared for. It turned out that the very plane this man of God was supposed to travel in crashed, and all the passengers died! If this man had not prayed and listened to God during and after his prayer, he would have gone to this good event – and he would have died. This would have been sleeping the sleep of death that would have caused unnecessary premature death.

This narrated story is a great example of "not everything good is permissible for the believer." Something may be good, but it may not be good for you due to other plans of God for your life. Remember when the Lord took the three disciples, Peter, James, and John, to watch with Him in prayers? The specific instruction that Jesus gave these three disciples was, *"Stay here and stay awake and keep watch with me"* (Matthew 26:38). Prayer is a very powerful tool that helps you sort out and differentiate what God wants you to do or not to do. Do not leave home daily without praying. May God help us all from sleeping the sleep of death.

11. Be Sensitive, Alert, and Vigilant (Watch and Pray!)

Another way to avoid sleeping the sleep of death is to be sensitive, alert, and vigilant. To be sensitive, alert, and vigilant, in a nutshell, refers to being spiritually disciplined and cautious at all times. One of the things believers are likened to is being a soldier Soldiers go through rigorous training and exercises to discipline themselves so they do not get careless and fall into the hands of their opponents. Soldiers are vigilant and very watchful. Jesus said believers should watch and pray to avoid falling into temptations from evil ones. In the book of Matthew 26:41, Jesus said, *"Watch and pray."* You need to know that God wants us to be spiritually conscious, sensitive, and cognizant of the happenings around us.

Jesus told His disciples in Matthew 26:41 (NIV), *"***⁴¹** **Watch and pray** *so that you will not fall into temptation. The spirit is willing, but the flesh is weak."* The same instruction still applies to us as Jesus' disciples. Many times, believers do the latter part and will completely ignore the first word: WATCH! For a believer to avoid being slothful in the Spirit, you must engage in the combination of the ministries of watching and praying.

In one of the previous chapters of this book, I narrated the story of the married Christian lady who, out of pity, offered her basement apartment to her high school friend and how she was a very prayerful but "unwatchful" Christian. This nice but slothful Christian lady was married for years without any child from her union with her husband. The lady's job took her away from her house at least five days a week because she worked during the night shift on her job. Of course, this dear Christian lady's ungodly friend ended up being pregnant by her friend's husband.

While I am not casting any stone at this Christian lady, the mathematics did not compute at all! How would you offer a free apartment to a single lady when you are married, and you were hardly home at night? Though it is very good for us as Christians to help people as our Lord has admonished, you must watch and pray. Do not watch without praying, and do not pray without watching. These two are twins; they go hand in hand.

Two examples in the Bible that we can emulate are:

- ***Abraham's covenant with God***

    "*^{10}Abram brought all these to him, cut them in two, and arranged the halves opposite each other; the birds, however, he did not cut in half. ^{11} Then birds of prey came down on the carcasses, but Abram drove them away." (Genesis 15:10-11, NIV)*

At this point in Abraham's life, he was entering a covenant that would shape his life and all his descendants. The man was not just following and obeying God's instructions; he was also sensitive enough to drive away the birds of prey. Some slothful Christians may leave the birds to linger and may think it was part of the covenant. Abraham did not sleep the sleep of death; he was not slothful, and he knew what to do at the right time by driving away the intruders.

- *Rebuilding the wall of Jerusalem by Nehemiah (Nehemiah 4:1-23)*

The work was significantly attacked, and Nehemiah and the laborers both watched and prayed. In verses 7-9 (NIV) and 21-23 (NIV), in fact, throughout the entire chapter, you will see the combination of watching and praying.

> *"7 But when Sanballat, Tobiah, the Arabs, the Ammonites, and the people of Ashdod heard that the repairs to Jerusalem's walls had gone ahead and that the gaps were being closed, they were very angry. 8 They all plotted together to come and fight against Jerusalem and stir up trouble against it. 9 But we prayed to our God and posted a guard day and night to meet this threat."*
>
> *"21 So we continued the work with **half the men holding spears, from the first light***

> *of dawn till the stars came out. ²² At that time I also said to the people, "**Have every man and his helper stay inside Jerusalem at night, so they can serve us as guards by night and as workers by day.**" ²³ Neither I nor my brothers nor my men nor the guards with me took off our clothes; each had his weapon, even when he went for water."*

In Nehemiah chapter 4, you will understand better how to be on guard effectively, so Satan and his messengers will not gain access into your life, family, and the work of your hands. In the Scriptures above, the words and sentences in bold inscription showed how Nehemiah and his team did not just pray, but they backed up their prayers with actions to resist their attackers.

Other Scriptures admonishing believers to be alert include:

- **1 Peter 5:8 (AMP)** - *"⁸ Be sober [well balanced and self-disciplined], be alert and cautious at all times. That enemy of yours, the devil, prowls around like a roaring lion [fiercely hungry], seeking someone to devour."*

- **2 Timothy 2:4 (AMP)** - *"⁴ No soldier in active service gets entangled in the [ordinary business] affairs of civilian life; [he avoids them] so that he* *may please the one who enlisted him to serve."*

12. Pray in the Spirit

Praying in the Spirit happens when the believer yields to the Holy Spirit by speaking in tongues. Speaking in tongues has many advantages; one of the advantages is that the believer is edified and empowered (1 Corinthians 14:4). The main way I believe speaking in tongues will help you to avoid being slothful and falling into the traps of the enemy is to make speaking in tongues a lifestyle. Do not limit speaking in tongues only to when in the building called church or when the pastor directs the church to pray in tongues. Do not limit "tonguing your heavenly language" to when you are praying privately.

I have made speaking in tongues a lifestyle by speaking in tongues almost all the time when I am alone. I speak in tongues while cooking, shopping, and driving, I speak in tongues instead of thinking negative thoughts or being idle. When I find myself in shopping malls, I start to speak in tongues and ask the Holy Spirit to empower me against impulsive buying. This is part of what Ephesians 6:18 means when it says, *"pray in the Spirit on all occasions."*

As you step out, pray in your understanding and ask for the grace to overcome slothfulness in the Spirit. Declare that you are sensitive in the Spirit and that you will not sleep the sleep of death. After praying in your understanding, ask the Holy Spirit to help you emphasize this prayer point and all other necessary prayers as you speak in tongues. Then, go ahead and begin to speak in tongues.

CHAPTER TWELVE

Special Prayers Against the Sleep of Death

SECTION ONE

DAILY VICTORY PRAYERS FOR SPIRITUAL ALERTNESS

1. Oh Lord, my Father, I thank You, for You have come to give me abundant life (John 10:10b). Based on this verse, I draw life from the life of God. There is no sleep of death in the abundant life Jesus came to give me, so as I step out today and do my daily activities, I will not become a victim of the sleep of death.

SPIRITUAL SLUMBER

2. I pray, in Jesus' name, that I will be spiritually alert as I go from place to place today. As Jesus did not sleep the sleep of death, I will not sleep the sleep of death on this day of the Lord. I will be spiritually alert and not fall into the traps of the enemy, in Jesus' name.

3. I pray according to Psalm 91:5b: I am not afraid of the arrow that flies by day. Arrows may fly, but in the name of Jesus, they will not come near me, and they will not come near my loved ones in Jesus' name. (You can pray specifically for your loved ones and mention their names.)

4. Oh Lord, my Father, thank You for being with me all day. As I lay down to sleep, I affirm that the Word of God in Psalm 127:2 will speak loud and clear over my life. I am the beloved of the Lord, and tonight, God will give me sweet dreams and sleep in Jesus' name. I declare that my sleep will be enjoyable, and my dreams will be lovely.

5. As I lay down to sleep, in the name of Jesus, I bind all terrors of the night. None will be able to come near me or any of my loved ones. I bind satanic day and night operators according to Psalm 91:5; they will not be able to carry out their evil assignments. I cancel and nullify all satanic night assignments and agendas in Jesus' name.

6. I declare right now that I will not sleep the sleep of death, either during the day or at night. I cover my life with the blood of Jesus. No evil will befall me day and night. During the day, I am barricaded with the blood of Jesus, and at night, my sleep and dreams are sweet, and my life is sweet. I will not sleep the sleep of death in Jesus' name. Amen!

SECTION TWO

NIGHT WATCH PRAYERS FOR SUPERNATURAL PRESERVATION

1. Father, in the name of Jesus, I thank You for being my shield and rock of protection. I thank You for the gift of salvation and the gift of life, and I ask for mercy in all areas where I have sinned against You and against the people You created. I appreciate You for the revelation of this subject—the sleep of death—and I pray in Jesus' name that as I sleep tonight, my sleep will be sweet. I refuse and reject any form of the sleep of death. I soak my bed, room, doors, and windows from the foundation to the rooftop of this house in the blood of Jesus.

2. I cancel all agendas of darkness. I bind satanic night and day messengers and operators. I pray for my spirit to be ready and combative against any attack, assault, or manipulation from any sleep invader. I

bind familiar spirits and enemies that pose as friends to confuse me in my sleep. I pray Psalm 3:5 and Proverbs 3:24, respectively, upon my life, and I will testify when I wake up that my sleep was sweet and peaceful because God sustained me in my sleep.

I pray all of these in the name of Jesus Christ. Amen!

SECTION THREE

PRAYERS FOR DIVINE LEADING

1. Oh Lord, my Father, please help me not to sit when my counterparts are seeking.

2. Oh Lord Jehovah, when others are being selected to the next levels of life or career, help me not to be told to sit.

3. In Jesus' name, I must always be among those who are chosen for good things.

4. In the name of Jesus, I pray today that as I go in and out of this place and even as I sleep, the Holy Spirit of God will guide me to be sensitive to the things happening around me.

5. Holy Spirit, please teach me to hear Your voice. When You are giving me a red light, help me not to ignore it and keep walking into danger.

6. I pray after the order of Exodus 13:21 that, as the fire by night and the pillar of cloud by day were a form of green and red light respectively for the Israelites, I will not break spiritual laws.

7. Help me, Jehovah, to obey spiritual traffic laws.

8. Oh Lord, I pray, just as the Israelites stopped at the pillar of cloud by day (a red light, saying "STOP") and moved by the pillar of fire at night (a green light, saying "Go"), Holy Spirit, teach me to see, recognize, and obey the red lights of the Spirit realm.

9. I will be sensitive to the green lights and red lights of God. I will hear the "stop" and the "proceed" from God in Jesus' name.

10. I bind every attempt of the enemy to confuse me.

11. I bind every plan of Satan to deceive or distract me by inviting me to go on red lights and to stop at God's green lights.

12. On this day of the Lord, I affirm Psalm 23 over my life (and the lives of my loved ones). The Lord is my shepherd, and as a good shepherd leads the sheep to still waters, He will lead me to still waters today. God will lead me to peaceful places, peaceful people, and peaceful events. By the leadings of God, I decree and declare that I will not be in places of trouble. Troublemakers are removed from my paths today,

in Jesus' name.

13. The disciples were insensitive to the Words of Jesus. Father, I will not sit down engaging in unprofitable things when I should be seeking You in prayer.

14. I will not sleep the sleep of death because God anoints my ears to hear and my mouth to speak. I will hear correctly and be spiritually alert and sensitive to act as a child of God.

15. Oh Lord, my Father, open my eyes of understanding to areas where I have been sleeping the sleep of death.

16. In the name of Jesus, I receive the power of God and fresh fire from the Holy Spirit to stay alert and prayerful.

17. I reject the heaviness of eyes in my place of prayer. I bind the spirit of slumber, and I will not sleep the sleep of death, in Jesus' name. I decree, in Jesus' name, that none of my family members will engage in the sleep of death.

18. Oh Lord, my Father, I receive the grace not to denounce Jesus. I will not denounce, deny, or desert Jesus in Jesus' name.

19. In Jesus' name, I refuse the sleep of death in all ramifications. I will be spiritually alert to the things of my life and those about my loved ones. The disciples could not watch with Jesus. Oh Lord, I receive the grace to stand in the gap for my loved ones and myself. I reject the sleep of slumber concerning my loved ones, and I will not sleep the sleep of death concerning my life, in Jesus' name.

20. Oh Lord, my Father, I will not invest in the wrong ventures, wrong careers, or wrong people. I will not be a wasted investment for the Lord. I receive grace to yield dividends of 100-fold, 1,000-fold, and exceedingly abundant folds in Jesus' name.

21. I will not sleep the sleep of death. I will not respond wrongly, react sharply, or run away from my position of greatness.

22. I decree and declare that none of my friends and family will be left behind in the great happenings of life. We will not be left behind. Whatever God is doing in the seasons of life will not elude us. I reject being left behind when others are called to higher and greater things.

23. I affirm that I will not be swept away by the sleep of death. I will be called to higher levels, and I pray that at my mountaintop experiences, I will not suffer from "heavy eyes syndrome." I pray and affirm the

Word of God upon my life. As Jesus did everything that He saw His Father do, so shall it be for me. I will not sleep when God is expecting me to watch and pray.

PRAYERS FOR DIVINE PROTECTION

(from consequences, danger, and the sleep of death)

1. I pray on this day, just as the disciples left behind by Jesus slept the sleep of death, I (mention your name or the names of your loved ones) will not experience the sleep of death.

2. In the name of Jesus, as the walls surround Jerusalem, so the Lord surrounds me (mention who and what you want God to surround) (Psalm 125:2). I affirm Zechariah 2:5 over my household and declare that the Lord is a wall of fire around us day and night; our present and future are in God's hands, in the name of Jesus.

3. My Father and my God, by the authority in the name of Jesus, I uproot any evil sown into my life as a result of the sleep of death. (Pray this for your loved ones who may be suffering as a result of the enemy's works.)

4. Oh Lord, my Father, please arise and help me and my family. Wherever we have slept the sleep of

death in the past and are suffering the consequences, Lord, arise in Your power and put a stop to all the consequences of the sleep of death in Jesus' name.

5. The disciples eventually suffered the consequences of the sleep of death. I pray in the name of Jesus that if there is any way the enemy is waiting to sift me or any of my loved ones as a result of sleeping the sleep of death, intervene so our future will not be affected by the sleep of death. Nobody in my family will be sifted, struck, stopped, or buffeted by the evil one.

SECTION FOUR

PRAYERS FOR SPIRITUAL ALERTNESS AND DESTINY PRESERVATION

1. I pray that you will not sleep the sleep of slumber. You will not be so sound asleep physically and become so insensitive spiritually that good and great things are stolen from your life.

2. As you read this book, may God, who gave me this revelation, give you spiritual alertness and sensitivity to ward off swappers of destinies and evil exchangers.

3. I decree and prophesy into your life that good and great things, good and fantastic visions, good and

great people will not be removed or taken from their places beside you.

Pray this next prayer aloud:

4. In the name of Jesus, as Mary sensed that it was time for Jesus to step into His ministry, I receive Mary's sensitivity to the happenings of my life and that of my family in Jesus' name (John 3). I will not be spiritually insensitive to the events happening around me.

5. Oh Lord Jehovah, I receive the alertness of Abraham. As Abraham drove away evil birds that were going to eat up his sacrifices, I am alert at all times to barricade God's blessings upon my life and my family members in Jesus' name.

6. In Jesus' name, the good things belonging to me will not be intentionally or carelessly given to another owner.

7. Oh Lord, my Father, I pray that this very year, all the good things belonging to me that have been stolen or swapped or are still hanging in the air will be delivered speedily in Jesus' name.

8. Oh Lord Jehovah, I pray Your Word, according to Proverbs 21:1, "that the hearts of the rulers of this world are in Your hands." I pray that as Solomon was alert to give sound judgments, Lord, motivate

the rulers, supervisors, leaders, politicians, and all people along the way of my life to do me good and not evil all the days of my life.

9. I pray that the gifts, talents, and resources God has given me will not be carelessly smothered or killed by me.

10. In Jesus' name, I and my loved ones will not misuse, abuse, or mismanage the resources of talents, treasures, time, and people the Lord has endowed us with.

11. Oh Lord, my God, I pray that I will not labor in vain. This prostitute went through a lot before delivering the baby she smothered through the sleep of death. My Lord and my God, I will not sleep the sleep of death. I will not labor and kill the fruits of my labor.

12. I refuse, renounce, and reject whatever makes people labor but stops or prevents them from reaping the harvests of their labors in the name of Jesus.

13. I stand in my authority as a child of God and bind demonic spirits behind wasted efforts.

14. I rebuke, in the name of Jesus, demonic spirits that make people labor and choke the harvests of labor. My labor will not be in vain. My harvests are plentiful. After the orders of Luke 5 and Psalm 23, I receive

cups running over and net-breaking experiences from the labor of my hands.

15. I pray, dear reader, that the wind of God blows such evil people away from all of us in Jesus' name. Peradventure, any reader has this tendency of "being quick to do evil and slow to do good," may the same wind of God uproot and flush the tendencies out of you in Jesus' name.

16. I pray by the authority in the name of Jesus that you will not major in minor and insignificant things. You will not spend your time, talents, and treasures chasing shadows.

17. In Jesus' name, receive the grace of rightness—the grace to do the right things at the right times, with the right people, in the right places, and achieve the right results in Jesus' name.

18. Oh Lord, my Father, where I am "birding" and flocking with birds with short feathers—people with short visions or no visions—intercept and redirect my paths. I will not shortchange my life.

19. Father, in the name of Jesus, remove anyone or any program in my life that can mar my destiny instead of making my destiny.

20. Oh Lord, You know the hearts of all people. Surround me and connect me with destiny builders,

not destiny destroyers. I rebuke and reject destiny swappers, destiny vandalizers, destroyers, users, and abusers in Jesus' name.

21. Oh Lord Jehovah, surround me with the right groups of people. Surround me with the three levels of right relationships:

    - Connect and surround me with people at higher levels of life who will help make my destiny beautiful, fruitful, and impactful. I receive them as my helpers of destiny. Help me to forever appreciate and celebrate their goodness in my life. Help me not to be a user; help me not to use and forget such helpers in Jesus' name.

    - Oh Lord, my Father, I pray that You also surround me with friends and contemporaries—people who are at the same level as me—friends that we can engage in healthy competitions of building each other's lives. I reject friends with crab mentality—those who will want to pull me down for only them to rise and shine in life in Jesus' name.

    - Oh Lord, my Father, in this race of life, please send along my path people who are below the level that I am. Please use me and every gift You have given me to help them climb the ladder of success. Lord Jehovah, deliver me from those who will use me to rise and forget how You have used me in their lives. I reject those who repay evil for good in Jesus' name.

22. Oh Lord, my Father, I thank You for Your Word. Thank You for revealing the deep things of Your Word to me. I thank You for Your Holy Spirit that lives in me. I thank You also for the power in the blood and the name of Jesus. As I engage in destiny-changing prayers, I plead the blood of Jesus all over my life. I decree and declare a turn of events to make my life better, brighter, and bigger in Jesus' name.

DELIVERANCE FROM THE SPIRIT OF SLUMBER AND SPIRITUAL BLINDNESS

1. In the name of Jesus, I come against the spirit of slumber, which is the sleep of death.

2. I decree and declare, peradventure I have been sleeping the sleep of death, not knowing what I should know. From this day, I receive my liberty. I call forth my destiny to arise and begin to shine like the stars in the name of Jesus.

3. In the name of Jesus, I stand on the authority of the name of Jesus—the name above all principalities and powers. I raise the banner of the blood of Jesus against destiny vandalizers, manipulators, switchers,

and killers. The Bible says, "Whatever I bind on earth is bound in heaven, and whatever I loose on earth is loosed in heaven." In Jesus' name, I bind evil spirits, dream invaders, satanic night operators, and everything Satan uses to manipulate the sleep of death in Jesus' name.

PRESERVATION OF DESTINY AND DIVINE PROTECTION

1. In the name of Jesus, whatever represents babies in my life is barricaded with the blood of Jesus. I soak my life, destiny, career, building project, business, and all the blessings of God in my life in the blood of Jesus. My present and future are soaked in the blood of Jesus. I decree henceforth, none will be able to manipulate or reconfigure my destiny in Jesus' name.

2. By the authority in the name of Jesus, I will not sleep the sleep of death like the careless prostitute. I will not be careless in my sleep. I reject the spirit of carelessness and the spirit of error.

3. I reject evil swapping, stealing, and vandalizing of destinies. I decree and declare that my destiny and the destinies of my loved ones will not be stolen, swapped, vandalized, or covered in Jesus' name. May God arise and be a barricade of fire around my

destiny in Jesus' name.

4. The wicked prostitute represents friendly enemies in someone's life. Father, in the name of Jesus, arise, expose, and expel enemies masquerading as friends in my life.

5. I decree and speak to my spirit (mention your name or names of loved ones): Arise, oh my spirit. I will not sleep the sleep of death. I will not fight the wrong battles. In Jesus' name, I will not fight my friends and embrace my enemies.

6. Oh Lord of glory, dear Holy Spirit of the Almighty God, the Bible says, "You will guide me and show me things to come." Dear Holy Spirit, anoint and open my eyes to see what I have been blinded to. Help me to know what I need to know. Anoint my ears to hear and my mind to perceive the spiritual truths behind the issues of my life in Jesus' name (John 16:13).

7. In the name of Jesus, I decree that my eyes of understanding are opened. I will see people for who they are, and I will have a discerning spirit to know good from evil and friends from enemies in Jesus' name.

PROTECTION OF VISION AND GOD-GIVEN IDEAS

1. In the name of Jesus, my "babies" (such as ideas, innovations, inventions, and vision) will not die. I will not sleep, kill, or smother the ideas and the opportunities God is giving to me. I pray in the name of Jesus that the ideas and visions God is downloading into my spirit will not remain as suggestions; they will not remain dormant without any actions to actualize them.

WARFARE AGAINST LAZINESS, PASSIVITY, AND SATANIC ARRESTERS

1. As Elijah called forth fire to burn those who went to arrest him in 2 Kings 1:10 & 12, I call forth fire to burn the arresters of destiny and instruments of the sleep of death in my life. I arrest such things as laziness, procrastination, lack of seriousness, slothfulness, and loving to sleep wastefully in Jesus' name.

2. In the name of Jesus, I, ... (mention your name), arise by the power of the Holy Spirit after the order of Isaiah 52:1–2. I put on the strength of God, so I decree and declare that the uncircumcised, destiny destroyers, and instruments of the sleep of death, will no longer come near me. I shake off the dust

and consequences of the sleep of death. I break all chains and shackles that tie people down and blind them with the sleep of death. I am no longer your candidate. I affirm the Word of God in John 8:36: I am free indeed by the Lord Jesus.

RESTORATION OF WHAT WAS STOLEN

1. Father, in the name of Jesus, as You used Solomon to restore the stolen child, raise the "Solomons" and restorers of this world to restore good things stolen in my life in Jesus' name.

2. In Jesus' name, make me the "Solomons" in other people's lives; make me an agent of restoration. I decree and affirm Isaiah 58:12 over my life that I am a rebuilder, raiser, restorer, and repairer of other people's lives in Jesus' name.

3. *(You can engage in being a "Solomon" for others by praying for those around you who might be going through a series of spiritual attacks and problems.)*

4. After the order of Isaiah 42:22, I stand in the gap for my loved ones going through spiritual vandalization, delays, swapping, covering, or stealing of their destinies. I stand in the gap for any of my loved ones trapped in the holes of wickedness, locked down in spiritual prisons. I declare: Anyone who has been held as prey, you are free now in the name of Jesus.

I decree and declare restoration into the lives and destinies of my loved ones. I stand upon the Rock, Christ the Redeemer, and I shout—restore, restore, restore—let there be restoration of good things that have been stolen in my life, in the lives of my loved ones, business, ministry, and family in Jesus' name.

DESTRUCTION OF EVIL FOUNDATIONS AND ALTARS

1. I use the authority in the name of Jesus to demolish and destroy evil altars, foundational problems, and ancestral evil patterns that may be causing problems in my life and the lives of my loved ones in Jesus' name.

2. I call forth the fire of God to fall and burn to ashes incantations, conjurations, and evil powers behind any family problems. I render the powers of satanic day and night operators useless and ineffective in my family in Jesus' name.

SECTION FIVE

PRAYERS FOR DESTINY PRESERVATION

1. In the name of Jesus, I will not play with my destiny.

2. I pray my deliverer will not be a grinder of grains in the name of Jesus.

SECTION SIX

PRAYERS FOR ESCAPE FROM DEATH TRAPS AND FULFILLMENT OF DESTINY

1. I pray for you, dear reader, that as David was spiritually sensitive to the evil environment around Saul, may God cause you to be alert in the Spirit to the happenings and the people around you.

2. You will escape every thought, arrow, and wish of death. As the spear of Saul missed the head of David, all evil arrows will miss you and your loved ones.

3. Saul wanted to pin David to the wall; instead, it was his instrument that went into the wall. The instrument of death intended for you will miss your head, your address, and its intended targets.

4. I decree a back to the sender to all enemies of your

life in Jesus' name.

5. As David escaped these death traps, I pray that you will escape death traps. Arrows of death will miss your head.

6. As David killed two hundred Philistines, you will escape assignments and plots of death.

7. David also escaped sleeping on the bed of death. Your bed, which is for comfort, shall never become a bed of death.

8. In the name of Jesus, as David escaped the seat of death, you will not sit on the wrong chair. Any chair meant for your death will never be occupied by you. Chairs of death will forever be empty after the orders of 1 Samuel 20:5 & 7 in Jesus' name.

9. I decree and declare that you will always outdo, outsmart, and outshine all your enemies in the name of Jesus.

David, although he was anointed to become king, was running from cave to cave with the hot pursuits of his enemies behind him. The Bible says God did not put David in the hands of Saul. 2 Samuel 5:12 (AMP) says, "And David knew that the LORD had established him as king over Israel and that He had exalted his kingdom for His people Israel's sake." Despite all of Saul's attempts to kill David so he would not be king, Saul failed. David was unstoppable and could not be killed by him. God's promise and plan for David to be king prevailed over all his enemies' evil plots and plans. I pray for you:

10. God's promises for your life shall all speedily come to pass.

11. You will be who God destined you to be.

12. As God settled and established David as king over Israel, God will enthrone you as a champion in the work of your hands.

13. God will establish your destiny, and your business will be established.

14. David escaped all avenues of death; you will escape all satanic traps and your enemies' plots of death.

15. By the authority in the name of Jesus, I decree and declare that you are unstoppable, unshakable, unsinkable, unbreakable, and unkillable.

16. Saul's daughter, Michal, helped David to escape the bed of death. I pray the friends and relatives of your enemies will deflect to help you against their person (1 Samuel 19:11–17; The Benjamites, Saul's kin, defected to help David – 1 Chronicles 12:16–18).

17. Michal, Saul's daughter, helped David against Saul. Jonathan, Saul's son, helped David against his father. The Benjamites, Saul's relatives, joined forces with David. I pray that everything God has created

will help you ascend the throne God has for you in life. The children, kinsmen, and kinswomen of your enemies will travel extra miles to be assets and helpers of destiny to you.

18. I pray, standing after the order of the angel in Revelation 10:2, with my right leg stationed on the sea and my left leg stationed on the land and a lifted hand, I decree by the power of God who lives forever and ever and created and owns the world and heavens, in the name of Jesus, you will not sleep on the beds of death nor sit on the chairs of death, nor enter the planes of death, nor travel in the trains of death, nor enter the vehicles of death. You will not travel on the roads of death nor stay in the cities of death. You will not be in the neighborhoods of death.

19. God, your Father, will silence all evil informants of your movements. The Bible says, "Evil speakers will not be established in the land." In the name of Jesus, God will shut the mouths of evil speakers against your life. Their lies and evil assignments will not be established in Jesus' name. You shall look for them and find them no more in Jesus' name (Psalm 140:11).

20. May all monitoring devices being used to monitor

your movements catch fire and burn to ashes in the name of Jesus.

21. All evil arrows aimed at you or any of your loved ones will return to sender. No arrow will befall you nor come near your dwelling in the name of Jesus.

22. Evil arrows of the wicked will miss your head and miss your address.

23. As David moved from being a shepherd boy and an errand boy and moved from cave to cave to the throne prepared for him as king, God will move you from whatever level you are to a higher dimension in Jesus' name.

24. David got to his place of knowing in 2 Samuel 5:12, where he knew he was established as king. In the name of Jesus, God will help you and lift you to your place of knowing—a place of establishment, a place of knowing, your throne of promise, and your place of manifestations of God's plans for your life.

25. Psalm 56:9 (NLT) says, "My enemies will retreat when I call to you for help. This I know: God is on my side." I pray that all your enemies will turn back from pursuing you. May God frustrate them.

26. As God sent a message of war to Saul when he was about to catch David, I pray, may God engage your

enemies with emergencies that will occupy them for the next 29 years of their lives in Jesus' name.

27. David called the place in 1 Samuel 23:28 – the Rock of Escape. By the God who lives forever, you and your loved ones are hidden under the Rock, and you have escaped forever in Jesus' name.

28. I pray for this reader, may God (the Changer of Seasons and Times) set up emergencies against all your enemies (1 Samuel 23:27). The Changer of Times and Seasons changed the season of David's life. David stopped running from cave to cave and ascended the throne God promised him. So shall it be for you in Jesus' name.

29. As Saul had a serious emergency at home, may your enemies have die-hard emergencies that will occupy them for a long time.

30. May God change your current season of life to a time of light and glory of God. May God change and establish all that pertains to you. May God establish your marriage, marital status, career, business, health, and all of your heart's desires in Jesus' name. Amen!

SECTION SEVEN

PRAYERS FOR FAMILY CONSECRATION AND SPIRITUAL ALERTNESS

1. Father, in the name of Jesus, help me not to experience the sleep of death.

2. Eli's family fell from grace to grass. On my watch, oh Lord, my family will not fall, fail, or falter. I reject falling from grace to grass by the authority in the name of Jesus. Through my obedience and alertness to the things of God, my family will move from grace to grace and glory to glory in Jesus' name.

3. Father, in the name of Jesus, the children in my family will not dishonor God. I pray for the reverential fear of God upon them.

4. After the order of Isaiah 11:2, I pray that the seven-fold Spirit of God will be upon the children in my family in Jesus' name (mention names of children).

5. They receive, after the order of Isaiah 11:2:

    - The Spirit of the Lord
    - The Spirit of Wisdom
    - The Spirit of Understanding
    - The Spirit of Counsel

- The Spirit of Strength
- The Spirit of Knowledge, and
- The Spirit of the fear (reverential fear and obedience) of the Lord in Jesus' name.

6. I reject the sin of Eli's children in this family. My children, and the children I intercede for, will not be carefree nor play down the things of God. I pray that after the order of Isaiah 11:3, these children's greatest joy will be to obey God in Jesus' name.

7. The sons of Eli were described in 1 Samuel 2:12 as worthless, dishonorable, and unprincipled men who did not know God nor respect Him. Father, I forbid and reject worthless, dishonorable, unprincipled children who will work for God but not walk with Him. My children will be honorable, respectful, and principled people who will walk and work for God in Jesus' name.

8. Lord, as a parent (caregiver, mother, or elder in the church), may I not commit the sin of Eli. Lord, help me to honor you above all others. I will not turn the other eye where I see my loved ones dishonoring God or the things of God in Jesus' name.

9. Father, in Jesus' name, I pray Ezekiel 36:26 (and Ezekiel 11:19–20) for me and my loved ones. Let Your Word be fruitful in my life and the lives of my

loved ones. Oh Lord, please, remove every stubborn, rock and stony heart from all of us. Thank You for giving us the hearts of flesh—hearts that are tender, responsive, obedient, and sensitive to Your voice, Word, and touch, according to Your Word in Ezekiel 36:26 (AMP): "Moreover, I will give you a new heart and put a new spirit within you, and I will remove the heart of stone from your flesh and give you a heart of flesh."

10. Oh Lord, I pray **Deuteronomy 30:6** over my family. Circumcise our hearts and the hearts of our seeds. Please, remove the desires to sin from our hearts, and help us and our descendants to love You with the totalities of our beings, in Jesus' name.

11. After the order of **Psalm 51:10**, oh Lord, create in me a clean heart—a new and loyal heart. Please, renew a right and steadfast spirit within me. I pray the same prayer over my seeds (mention names of your children or grandchildren).

12. After the order of **Jeremiah 32:39–41a**, Father, give me a heart that will reverently fear You forever. Put in my heart, oh Lord, Your fear and reverential awe of You. Help me to always turn to You and not turn away from You, in Jesus' name. Declare this prayer for your loved ones also.

13. In Jesus' name, **Matthew 13:8 & 23** is my portion

and the portion of my loved ones forever. My heart is the good soil. As the Word of the Lord comes into my heart, I will grasp and understand it, in Jesus' name. The Word will bear fruit and yield a hundred times what is sown, and produce harvests beyond my wildest dreams, in Jesus' name.

SECTION EIGHT

WARFARE PRAYERS TO REJECT THE SLEEP OF DEATH

1. I will not sleep the sleep of death. I reject the lot of the chief baker. Father, help me to be spiritually alert both in my dreams and while awake.

2. Father, I receive the alertness of Abraham after the order of **Genesis 15:11 (NIV)**, which says, *"Then birds of prey came down on the carcasses, but Abram drove them away."*

3. I refuse to go backward in life. The path of my life is like a shining light that shines brighter and brighter (**Proverbs 4:18**).

4. The baker moved from the palace to prison and then to the pole of death. I will not fall from grace to grass. I cancel all the plans of darkness to make me or any of my loved ones fall, fail, or falter.

5. The baker slept the sleep of death in the area of his career, and another baker took his place. In Jesus' name, nobody will take my place in my career, family, marriage, and every other aspect of my life. I reject the sleep of death concerning all areas of my life.

6. Evil birds ate up the good things carried by the baker. Father, in the name of Jesus, the good things of my destiny, life, and family will not be stolen, eaten, or vandalized by anyone.

7. I rebuke whoever or whatever is assigned to trouble my dreams or cause any damage in my life. Let the fire of God fall to burn and consume into ashes whatever represents evil birds, evil people, or any evil gadget assigned against my life, in Jesus' name.

8. In the name of Jesus, after the order of **Genesis 15:11**, I drive away evil birds, animals, and people masquerading to cause harm in my life. I drive away, by the power of the Holy Spirit and after the order of Abraham, anything or anyone trying to sabotage God's plans for my life, in Jesus' name.

9. Jesus drove away Satan in **Matthew 4:10b (AMP)**, which says, *"Then Jesus said to him, 'Go away, Satan!'"* In fact, the **NLT** version says, *"Get out of here, Satan."* I decree:

    - In the name of Jesus, get out of here, Satan!

- In the name of Jesus, get out of my family, Satan!
- Get out of my body, Satan, in the name of Jesus!
- In the name of Jesus, get out of my career!
- Away from me and my loved ones, Satan, in the name of Jesus!

10. I decree and declare that my spirit and the spirits of my loved ones are on alert—to be dangerous and destructive—and demolish all contrary spirits, in Jesus' name.

11. May God release assorted anointing, entrepreneurial grace, multidimensional grace, and opportunities for multiple sources of income upon my life and the lives of my loved ones, in Jesus' name. Amen!

FINAL DECLARATION OF VICTORY OVER THE SLEEP OF DEATH

1. In the name of Jesus, no more sleep of death in my life (mention your name or the names of your loved ones) from today. I receive the grace to be combative, aggressive, and destructive against any sleep invaders and satanic operators in Jesus' name.

2. I receive spiritual sensitivity and disallow all evil infiltrations into my life and the lives of my loved ones in Jesus' name. Amen!

CONCLUSION

As I conclude this book, I would like you to remember to fight spiritual slackness, spiritual slothfulness, and spiritual slumber at all times. Be spiritually sharp and sensitive to the things happening in your lives, families, environments, and the world at large because the days are evil. According to Romans 13:11:

AMPLIFIED VERSION:

"11 Do this, knowing that this is a critical time. It is already the hour for you to awaken from your sleep [of spiritual complacency]; for our salvation is nearer to us now than when we first believed [in Christ]."

MESSAGE VERSION:

"11 But make sure that you don't get so absorbed and exhausted in taking care of all your day-by-day obligations that you lose track of the time and doze off, oblivious to God."

NEW INTERNATIONAL VERSION:

"11 And do this, understanding the present time: The hour

has already come for you to wake up from your slumber because our salvation is nearer now than when we first believed."

From the Scriptures above, you can notice the choice of words, such as awaken from your sleep, wake up from your slumber, do not get so absorbed and exhausted, do not lose track of time, do not doze off, and do not be oblivious to the things of God.

As we stay awake, vigilant, and utilize the points mentioned in this book, we see that the devil may roar around all he wants, but the believer is trained to stump on the devil. You are to maximize the authority you have received as a believer and rise as the soldiers of Christ, show the **devil** that you cannot be **deceived** like Eve, **deflated** like Samson, **detoured** like Solomon, **defeated** like Saul, **destroyed** like Judas, **derailed** like Ananias and Sapphira. You will not **deny** Christ like Peter. I pray that we will not be **denied** the benefits we should receive in Christ. Believers have a better **"d"** than all the **"ds"** of the devil; Christ Jesus has **delivered** believers, and we refuse to sleep the sleep of **death.**

"¹⁵ ("Behold, I am coming like a thief. Blessed is he who stays awake and who keeps his clothes [that is, stays spiritually ready for the Lord's return], so that he will not be naked—spiritually unprepared—and men will not see his shame.")" (Revelation 16:15, AMP). Glory!

SPIRITUAL SLUMBER

www.ingramcontent.com/pod-product-compliance
Lightning Source LLC
Chambersburg PA
CBHW070552160426
43199CB00014B/2473